SHOCKING
SOMERSET STORIES

Jack W. Sweet

Somerset Books

First published in Great Britain in 1999

Copyright © 1999, Jack W. Sweet

British Library Cataloguing in Publication Data
A CIP record for this book is available from the British Library

ISBN 0 861834 90 9

SOMERSET BOOKS
Official publisher to Somerset County Council

Halsgrove House
Lower Moor Way
Tiverton EX16 6SS
Tel: 01884 243242
Fax: 01884 243325

Printed in Great Britain by MPG Ltd, Bodmin

CONTENTS

ABOUT THE AUTHOR

JACK SWEET was born in Yeovil and has lived most of his life in the town of many of his ancestors. An old boy of the former Yeovil School, he joined the staff of Yeovil Borough Council on leaving the Royal Air Force in 1958. After working as a professional local government administrator he took early retirement following thirty-four-years' service with the Borough Council and its successor the South Somerset District Council.

Jack Sweet has always had a great interest in history and has been writing articles for local publications, including the weekly *Yeovil Times* and South Somerset District Council's monthly *News and Views*. His first book *Shocking Somerset Murders of the Nineteenth Century* was published by Somerset Books in 1997.

In addition to his writing Jack Sweet is interested in family history, photography, voluntary work in the Museum of South Somerset, and visiting former battlefields in various parts of the world. He is married with three daughters and a grandson who takes up the rest of his time!

DEDICATION

To my wife Margaret for her patience and support and to my late
parents Reg and Edna Sweet, true Somerset folk.

Old Songs are best – how sweet to hear.
The strains of home and memory dear!
Old books are best – how tale and rhyme
Float with us down the stream of time!
Clarence Urmy (1858-1923)

ACKNOWLEDGEMENTS

My many thanks to Marion Barnes and Jennifer Wickes of the Museum of South Somerset, Paul Smith, Robin Ansell and Mrs Sheila Ewington of Yeovil Reference Library, and David Bromwich and staff of the Somerset Studies Library for their invaluable help during the preparation of this book.

To Michael Shorter, ARPS, for his great help in preparing many of the photographs.

To the Somerset Archive and Record Service for permission to reproduce my photograph of the Burial Register of the Parish of Stogursey (DP STOGS 2/1/8).

To the publishers of the *Visitor* and Martin Heal, Editor of the *Western Gazette*, for permission to reproduce the articles acknowledged in the Sources.

To *Somerset and Dorset Notes and Queries* for permission to reproduce 'The Devil's Drive' and 'Quantock Hills' Ghost.'

To Nigel J. Clarke Publications for permission to use the Luftwaffe Aerial Reconnaissance Photograph of Yeovil.

PHOTOGRAPHS

Copyright of all photographs belongs to the author unless shown below.
1, Somerset Archive and Record Service; 6, 12, 13, 16, 21, Museum of South Somerset; 2, 20, 22, Somerset County Council Library Service; 18, *Taunton Courier*; 8, 17, Somerset Archaeological and Natural History Society; 27, Nigel J. Clarke Publications.

INTRODUCTION

The stories in the following chapters occurred in Somerset in the pre-television age when the main sources of news were the papers or word of mouth and generally required imagination to visualise what had happened. From early days, editors realised that sensational stories which could shock, surprise and stimulate the imagination of their readers sold newspapers and therefore lurid detail and extensive coverage would be given to a 'good story.'

I have drawn on Somerset newspapers for many of my stories which occurred in the one hundred and fifty or so years before television pictures were beamed across our county and when editors and their journalists provided the words to stimulate our forebears' imaginations.

I hope, therefore, that in the stories which follow, I will be able to recreate some of the surprise and, in a few instances perhaps, a little of the sadness which the Somerset folk who read or heard about them felt in the days before yesterday.

THE LOSS OF THE
WILLIAM AND MARY

At about eight o'clock on the evening of Thursday, 23 October 1817, the regular Bristol to Waterford sailing packet, the *William and Mary*, commanded by Captain William Mauley, left the port of Pill and made her way down the River Avon. Once out in the Bristol Channel with a bright moon and a steady breeze from the north-east, all seemed set fair for the packet and her 56 passengers to reach the port in southern Ireland by the next evening.

The passengers, a cross-section of early nineteenth century society, included wealthy Pierse Barron, his four sisters and their manservant, returning home to the estate at Ballyneil, with their travelling coach lashed to the deck. There was a Roman Catholic priest, Father Giles, Mr Cliff, an Irish barrister, Mr Shortis, a Bristol businessman, Mrs Sandys, the wife of the Reverend Mr Sandys of Pilltown, County Waterford, and their younger daughter, Selina, and niece Jane Burroughs. Lieutenant Thebalier of the 95th Regiment of Foot, was travelling with his nineteen-year-old bride, the only daughter of Alderman Dennis of Waterford. Mr Snow was returning on half pay from his regiment which had left for garrison duty in St Helena, and labourers Cornelius Leary, James Kennedy, John Ryan and Florence Donovan were going home. Also on board was John Hayes, the mate of an American trading vessel.

The *William and Mary* had made good progress through the difficult waters at the mouth of the Avon, when at about ten o'clock Captain Mauley went below and assured the passengers that everything was in order and they could retire for the night. In the cabin, where fifteen of the more wealthy travellers were enjoying a little more comfort, Pierse Barron was reading to his nervous sisters, while in steerage, the passengers sought what comfort they could find in the dim, crowded hold. Lieutenant Thebalier, after seeing his wife safe in her berth in the cabin, sat down with a glass of whisky and water.

Captain Mauley came back on deck and, after setting the watch with the mate, John Outerbridge at the helm, retired below to snatch some sleep. About half an hour later, in almost perfect conditions, the *William and Mary* was making good passage between the island of Flat Holme and Lavernock Point when the ship shuddered and there was the groaning of tortured timbers: the *William and Mary* had run onto the Wolves rocks.

The Captain was rudely awakened by the shock and as he joined the frightened passengers on deck, he cursed the mate for a damned scoundrel as he realised what had happened The ship slipped off the reef but a quick inspection below found timbers sprung and water coming in. However, the *William and Mary* was less than two miles from the Welsh shore and a well-disciplined crew might have saved her by immediately manning the pumps and managing the sails. Tragically the packet's crew were not, and the steward with three crewmen made for the small rowing boat hanging over the stern.

Most of the passengers were in a state of extreme panic, but there were some cool heads. Lieutenant Thebalier placed his wife in the rowing boat and then went to see what he could do to help. However, there was no sense of 'women and children first' on the *William and Mary* and finding the young woman in their boat the sailors pushed her back on deck . The boat was lowered and, after picking up the mate, the crew rowed for the shore.

The helm was deserted and with the captain otherwise occupied in trying to save his ship, the vessel went out of control until John Hayes took the helm. Helped by some of the passengers managing the sails and with the captain and some passengers at the pumps or baling, Hayes began to ease the crippled packet towards the shore but the lack of experienced seamen was fatal. After about half an hour's struggle, the *William and Mary* suddenly went down stern first about a mile from Sully Island in six fathoms of water. As the sea poured across the deck, the passengers were swept shrieking and crying into the Bristol Channel. The four Barron sisters were last seen sinking entwined in each others' arms and the young wife of Lieutenant Thebalier was torn from his grasp. A soldier, his wife and baby made their way to the bows where they sat down and clinging to each other sank with the ship.

Although James Hayes' gallant efforts to reach the shore had failed, they had not been completely in vain, for he had brought the *William and Mary* from some 30 fathoms of water to six and, as she settled on the bottom about ten feet of top mast stood above the surface and the rigging became the refuge for fourteen survivors, including James Hayes and Lieutenant Thebalier

As the packet went under, Pierse Barron, Mr Shortis and Father Giles struck out for the shore but after a while Pierse Barron began to tire and despite encouragement from his fellow survivors cried out, 'I can go no further!' and sank from sight. Shortly afterwards the other two men were picked up by the packet's boat and so survived.

After clinging to the top mast rigging for over two hours, the four-teen survivors were finally rescued by a Pill yawl sent out when the mate and the crew reached land and raised the alarm. The survivors were taken to Cardiff where they were warmly received and a sub-scription was raised for those who had lost everything in the wreck.

Twenty-three passengers and crew survived the wreck of the *William and Mary* but all the women and children on board were drowned as was Captain Mauley, who left a widow and three chil-dren. Among the survivors was Lieutenant Thebalier and the four labourers who finally made it back to their native Ireland. The news of the disaster and the desertion of the crew was received with much alarm and great concern in Bristol and Waterford, and more so when allegations were made about the conduct of the mate just before the packet ran onto the Wolves.

On 3 November, Alderman Fripp of the Bristol Corporation, began to examine several of the survivors from the *William and Mary* who had returned to the city. The examinations were carried out individually and the first was the American seaman, John Hayes, who described the circumstances of the wrecking of the packet and how he had assisted Captain Mauley in trying to save the vessel. He had not seen the mate at the helm or at the pump and he believed that had the crew remained on board and worked the ship, all might have been saved.

John Heffernan, a recently discharged solder from the 53rd Regiment of Foot, stated that he had helped at the pump and in bal-ing. As he came on deck he saw the crew take to the boat and the helm was deserted. Another former soldier, Patrick Kelly, stated that he had been travelling with his brother and was below in steerage when the packet struck the rocks. He saw the mate leap overboard grasping a wooden spar and be picked up by the boat. Patrick Kelly recalled Captain Mauley shouting after the mate calling him a villain and said that the captain had remained at the pump until the last moment. He had tried to swim to the shore but was forced to turn back and found refuge in the rigging; his brother had drowned.

Alderman Fripp now adjourned the examinations until 6 November when Lieutenant Thebalier presented himself. The officer remembered Captain Mauley coming below and telling the passen-gers that all was well. When the *William and Mary* struck he had fol-lowed the captain up to the deck and saw the mate coming from the midships. He recalled hearing the Captain shout that the mate was a damned infernal scoundrel who could not be trusted for five minutes and he had lost the vessel. Lieutenant Thebalier described how he had gone below to calm the lady passengers but a sudden inrush of water into the cabin caused panic and everyone scrambled up the companionway. He had taken his wife back on deck and after placing her in the boat hanging at the stern, he had returned to give what help he could. The Lieutenant remembered seeing John Hayes at the helm and at the Captain's direction steer for the shore. He had not seen his wife pushed back on board and despite all his efforts to save her she had been swept from his arms.

The steward of the *William and Mary*, Daniel Maclachlan, was next examined and was perfectly honest in saying that he had taken to the boat to save his life. He believed the mate was at the helm when he came on deck but could not recall seeing a lady in the boat. The steward explained that the occupants of the boat had not offered to help as they feared it would be overwhelmed by passengers trying to save themselves.

A member of the crew, William Thomas, was next, and said that the mate was at the helm when the packet struck and that he remained there. He recalled getting into the boat and cutting it free. A lady had been placed in the boat and a sailor called Miller had told her to go back on board otherwise she might be drowned. The mate had been pulled from the sea about ten minutes after they left the packet. The boat had been difficult to manage as it was waterlogged and there was only one oar.

Last to be examined was the mate, John Outerbridge, who had been an able seaman on the 74 gun man-of-war, *HMS Centaur*. In addition to having been accused by some of the survivors of deserting the *William and Mary*, John Outerbridge was alleged to have been disporting himself with a woman in Mr Barron's coach when the packet struck the Wolves. He stated that the captain had given him the helm at about ten o'clock and later ordered him to steer to northward; shortly after the packet had gone on to the rocks. The mate stated that he had left the helm and gone forward to haul in the square sail, which was hindering the recovery of the vessel, after which he had hoisted the fore sail. Finding the American sailor at the helm he had gone to help with the pumping and baling. John Outerbridge stated that the woman with whom he was reported to have been 'romping' was a Mrs Taylor whose husband he knew in Waterford and she had asked him to look after her boxes. He strongly denied taking her into the coach.

The mate went on to claim that Captain Mauley had become so frightened that he had been incapable of giving directions for saving the packet and his last words were 'Oh Lord John, what shall I do!'

As the ship sank John Outerbridge stated that he had grabbed a spar and swam to the boat. After great difficulty, sculling with the one oar and constant baling, they had reached the shore and, finding a Pill yawl, had sent it out to rescue the survivors in the rigging. Throughout his examination the mate maintained that he had not deserted the helm and had worked to save the *William and Mary* until the end.

No further survivors were examined and on Saturday 15 November 1817, Felix Farley's *Bristol Journal* reported that Alderman Fripp had concluded his inquiry and it was found that:

> There was direct blame to be attached to those who had the command of the vessel, whether it is applied to the unfortunate man (the Captain) who perished, or the Mate who survives; there does not appear to be any rational cause for the accident; there is ground for imputing to the crew of the vessel a dereliction in their duty as British seamen, and consequently of a great breach of humanity, in leaving their post at so early a stage of the distress, and when their presence might have been most essentially useful. On the other hand, it must be allowed, that there is no proof of any act of wilful cruelty on the part of the men, nor of any conduct that may not be extenuated by that strongest of all pleas – self-preservation.

On 13 November, two days before the article appeared in the *Bristol Journal*, *The Times* reported that four labourers who had survived the wreck had sworn affidavits before the Mayor of Waterford that after the captain had gone below to rest, the mate had given the helm of the packet to one of the crew and taken a woman passenger into the coach lashed to the deck. The mate and the woman were still in the coach when the packet ran onto the rocks. But Alderman Fripp's inquiry had been concluded before the affidavits were signed and it was not re-opened. History appears silent on the future career of the mate of the ill-fated sailing packet *William and Mary*, John Outerbridge.

THE BRUTES OF BRIDGWATER

During the early years of the nineteeth century there were two kinds of apprentices – trade apprentices, who were voluntarily bound to a master craftsman to learn his trade, and pauper children known as poor apprentices who were put out by the Overseers of the Poor for service with tradesmen. In many instances the poor apprentices were treated little better than slaves, and maybe worse.

One particularly harrowing tale of the abuse of a poor apprentice took place in Bridgwater and came to a tragic conclusion on the morning of Monday, 20 January, 1823.

During the summer of 1822, a nine-year-old pauper child, William Bartlett, was apprenticed to William Hunt, a master chimney sweep of Bridgwater. The boy died on 20 January after a fortnight's illness but when a local surgeon, Mr J. Haviland, examined the small body he discovered signs of violence. An inquest was held and following a post mortem report and the evidence of continuous ill treatment, William Hunt and his wife, Mary, were charged with the wilful murder of their apprentice, William Bartlett, by repeated ill usage. The couple were brought to trial before the Honourable Sir James Burrough at the Somerset Assizes in Taunton on Monday, 1 April 1823 and both pleaded not guilty to the indictment.

The first and principal witness was thirteen-year-old John Clarke, a fellow poor apprentice of William Bartlett, who had agreed to give evidence only after he had been promised that he would be released from his apprenticeship, and he told a tale of horrible brutality. John stated that the two apprentices slept together on a bed of chaff with only a soot cloth for a cover. Their master had beaten William every other day, sometimes with a whip and often with his fists. From the hay-making season of 1822, when the boy had been bound apprentice, until his death, he had never had more than five or six shirts. William regularly dirtied himself at night and sometimes he had fouled his clothes. When this happened both the master and mistress would beat the boy and he was often naked during this torment. The instruments used during the beatings were then produced and the court saw an ash walking stick about an inch thick with a knob at the end, a donkey whip with a thong, and a particularly nasty looking implement made from three long strips of whalebone lashed together.

John Clarke resumed his testimony and told how the regular beatings took place all over the house, upstairs, down in the kitchen and out in the back yard and on numerous occasions William Bartlett had been naked. Just before Christmas, the boy had been tied by ropes to the banisters of the stairs for one whole day and night without food. On one of the coldest days in early January, because William had fouled himself, he was beaten from his bed and out into the yard where he had been plunged into the icy water of the pump trough and left for over half an hour. The brutality continued during the following days and reached its climax when Hunt had picked up the boy by his feet and slammed his head down on the brick floor and then beat him through the house. On the day before he died William had been very ill and when he would not eat his dinner Mrs Hunt had beaten him across his back. The boy had then dragged himself upstairs and into his bed where he died the following morning. John Clarke recalled that his mistress had put the corpse into her children's bed and then, because it was very dirty, she had made him carry it down to the coal hole. His evidence was now complete but before he left the witness box, John Clarke was allowed to show some wounds on his head which he said had been caused by Hunt.

Neighbour, Thomas Newbolt told the court that he had seen William Bartlett being beaten in the yard and heard Hunt shout out that he would be damned if he would not cut the boy to pieces if he did not stop dirtying himself. Newbolt's young daughter recalled seeing Hunt take the boy by his feet and throw him head first down on the floor after which William Bartlett had not moved for some time.

The last witness was Mr Haviland, the surgeon, who stated that the boy's body had been badly bruised and when he had opened it he had been shocked by the highly inflamed condition of the lungs and intestines. In his opinion, however, William Bartlett had died from inflammation of the lungs which might have been caused by cold and wet.

The surgeon's evidence was somewhat watered down from the testimony he had given at the inquest when he had said that it was his decided belief that the boy's death had been very much accelerated by ill usage and for want of proper sustenance. He was now saying that William Bartlett had died from natural disease and the abuse and starvation he had suffered had no material affect.

To gasps of disbelief and disgust from the crowded public gallery, the jury returned a verdict of not guilty, and the brutal pair left the dock, no doubt blessing their lucky stars that they were not heading for the scaffold or a long voyage in a convict ship to Australia for a long period of penal servitude.

Poor little William Bartlett, whose brief childhood had ended in the hell of abuse, beatings and starvation, finally lay in peace in his pauper's grave.

A LIFE LOST FOR A KISS

L ate on Thursday evening, 13 August 1857, George Taylor, the driver of the 'Leopold' railway engine fell from the train and was fatally injured. The *Western Flying Post* reported on the proceedings of the inquest, held two days later at the Nicoll Arms in Frome, and the story which emerged was a strange one.

Miles Handy, the fireman of the 'Leopold' railway engine, testified: 'On Thursday evening the deceased was driving his engine from Weymouth to Chippenham and when we were between Witham and Frome, the deceased told me to give a look out. I took hold of the regulator, and expected the deceased had gone back to the water tank, to see if it would carry us to Chippenham or not. I then looked to the water-gauge lamp, which had gone out, and I was bothering to light it, and keeping a look out as well when I heard the guard shout out saying George had fallen off. The guard was then on the tender. I shut off the steam, and whistled to the driver of the front engine telling him something had happened. [Two engines were hauling the train.] I then backed the engine and carriages by the guard's orders. I cannot describe the spot where the man lay: he was picked up and put in a second-class carriage, and brought to Frome. He was sensible and said 'My back is broke Miles,' two or three times. He did not tell me how he fell off. Taylor was on the engine when we left Bruton. The deceased and I had no dispute or words.'

Frederick Somers, the guard now gave evidence: 'I am guard on the Great Western Railway, and acted as such on Thursday to the ten o'clock train from Weymouth. We were rather late starting from Bruton that night. When we were about one mile from Witham, towards Frome, I saw the deceased fall from the tender against a wall and rebound against the carriage I was sitting in, which broke the panel of the door. I was leaning on the window of the carriage at the time. I endeavoured to stop the train as soon as possible, by blowing my whistle, and went along the tender and told the stoker. We went back and found the deceased by the side of Bull's Bridge, where he had fallen, he was sensible, he made no remark as to how the accident happened. The deceased was sober before leaving Weymouth and his mother had brought him some coffee. My brake was in the first carriage from the tender, about two yards.'

Mrs Sarah Fouraker testified: 'I am the wife of Thomas Fouraker, Inspector of the Exeter Police. On Thursday evening last I left Exeter for Frome, and stayed at Yeovil till the eleven o'clock train. After passing Bruton I saw a man on the steps of the carriage next to the tender. I was in the second carriage from the tender. He shortly afterwards looked into the carriage I was in and asked me if I wanted company, I said No. He then said there was no one in the next carriage and he would keep me company. He wanted to give me a kiss, I would not. He then wanted me to shake hands, I would not. He then went towards the door of the carriage I was sitting in, as if to leave, but returned several times, and wanted me to shake hands, but I persisted in not doing so, and kept my face out of the window because I would not look at him. I saw nothing more of the deceased till he was picked up from the bank on the left hand side of the train. He left the carriage on the right hand side. I did not then know who it was. When he was in the carriage with me he seemed very much frightened because I told him I should expose him. Shortly after he left the carriage the whistle blew, and the train was stopped. The deceased appeared to be sober, and not like a man who had been drinking.' When asked why she did not raise the alam, the witness replied: 'I was too much frightened to do so, and deceased did not use any violence towards me or push me, or make a noise.'

The last reported evidence came from Mr J. Portch who recalled: 'I was at Frome Station awaiting the arrival of the mail train from Weymouth when the first engine arrived and I heard that a man had fallen off the second engine or tender. I went for Dr White, and afterwards assisted in conveying the deceased to the Nicoll Arms where I stayed with him till his death, which took place at 1 o'clock on Friday morning.'

The jury returned a verdict of accidental death.

The *Somerset & Wilts Journal*, in commenting on the event, suggested that 'there ought to be some more speedy and effectual means of communicating between the driver and guard. The present system calls loudly for legislative interference, the Directors seeming blind to all that relates to the comfort and safety of travellers. Had there been, as in America, an entrance at the end of each carriage, with a public walk walk through to the tender, the present unhappy accident, by which a widow and two small children have to lament the death of their only support, would never have occurred. In this instance the guard was obliged, at the risk of his life, to get from the carriages to the tender while the train was going at the rate of forty miles per hour. We are informed that the usual expedient on the Great Western Railway for alarming the driver, is to put on the brakes, but in this instance there was only one guard in charge of the train.'

WESTON PIER
DESTROYED BY FIRE

Monday, 13 January 1930, was an unlucky day for Weston-super-Mare for just after 6.30pm the Grand Pier Pavilion caught fire and was totally destroyed.

'The huge red flames drew thousands of townspeople to the sea front at 6.45,' reported the *Western Gazette,* and readers were told that, 'the fire was first noticed by an ex-policeman who was walking along the front. He raised the alarm and within five minutes the local brigade were on the spot. It was obvious, however, that the pavilion was doomed for a strong wind fanned the flames, which gained a firmer hold every minute. The fire brigade was hampered from the beginning, for water was not available on the pier, and hoses had to be laid from the promenade a quarter of a mile away.

'The receding tide allowed spectators to get a near view of the blaze. Within a quarter of an hour the pavilion was enveloped in flames which were seen for many miles across the Mendips and along the Welsh coast, and one after the other the four domes of the pavilion crashed into the sea. Then the whole of the pavilion collapsed in a shower of sparks and was swallowed up by the waters.

'The fire fighters were forced back along the pier inch by inch, but finally were able to [take up a position] by the bandstand, and the pier from here to the promenade was saved. All that remains of the pavilion (which accommodated 2500 people) and the "fun fare" which was at the extreme end of the pier, are the steel girders sticking out of the water.

'The pier was constructed in 1904 at a cost of £120,000, the proprietors being the Weston-super-Mare Grand Pier Company, of which the Marquis of Bute was chairman, and Mr H. Broomfield, secretary and manager. Mr Broomfield was travelling by train from London to Weston-super-Mare while the fire was raging, and his wife was one of those who looked on from the promenade. This is a big blow to this popular seaside resort, where it was one of the main attractions of the town.

'The pavilion had not been occupied since the Christmas pantomime. Kubelik was due to play there next month and theatrical contracts had been entered into for the coming season. The amusement caterers on the pavilion have suffered a severe loss, one man losing £2000 worth of automatic machines.

'The cause of the outbreak is unknown.

'A woman staying at an hotel which faces the pier said that only the direction of the wind prevented the flames from spreading along the pier to buildings on the sea front. "The blaze was terrific, the flames leaping many feet higher than the surrounding buildings. It was a wonderful sight. The flames were reflected in the stormy water, and almost as far as the horizon the sea was like a mass of liquid fire."

'Many tons of burnt woodwork were washed ashore by Monday night's high tide, and on Tuesday morning children were in the mud beneath the pier scrambling for pennies which had come from the burst automatic machines. One of the safes from the pavilion was, on Tuesday morning, recovered in the mud beneath the wreckage. It was undamaged.

'Weston-super-Mare has two piers – the Grand Pier and the Old Pier. There was a serious fire many years ago at the Old Pier, which was subsequently rebuilt.'

THE SHOOTING AT THE ROCK HOUSE INN

To get up one morning looking forward to another normal day but by its end to be a murderer under the threat of the hangman's noose is the stuff of nightmare, but for James Pearce the nightmare was all too real.

When James Pearce, a twenty-seven-year-old hawker of pamphlets and song sheets, woke up on the morning of Friday, 20 May 1814, just another day was in prospect and when he called in at the Rock House Inn near Curry Mallet just before noon it is probable that nothing more than a pleasant drink and a little business was on his mind.

The afternoon and early evening passed pleasantly enough in the company of Thomas Burnell but as the hour was getting late the two men decided to stay for the night and the landlord, James Hellard, made up two beds for his customers. At about eight o'clock, a not-too-sober James Pearce decided to call it a day and take to his bed but as he made to leave the bar, the landlord called out that he owed for two pots of cider. Denying that he owed anything and with the liquor flowing through his veins, Pearce flew into a rage and lashed out at the landlord landing several nasty blows. However, James Hellard was used to dealing with the results of too much drink and knowing that he could get the money when his customer was sober the next morning, he made no further demand and everything calmed down. Suddenly Pearce became aggressive again and threatened to strike the landlord, who now realizing that something would have to be done, told the not-too-sober Thomas Burnell to restrain his drinking companion while he went to Curry Mallet to find the parish constable.

About an hour and a half later, James Hellard returned without the constable but carrying a pair of handcuffs. Pearce had quietened down but fearing another outbreak the landlord asked him to hold out his hands so that the cuffs could be snapped on and a peaceful night obtained thereby. It seemed at first that Pearce would comply and taking off his coat he held his hands out to be secured. The landlord, however, told him to put his coat back on because it would be cold to stay without a coat all night but Pearce flew again into a rage and lashed out at James Hellard who beat a hasty retreat from the bar.

Once again the bar quietened and Thomas Burnell fell asleep only to be suddenly brought back to consciousness by the loud crash of a gun shot. To his horror he saw Pearce sitting at one end of the bar, a smoking gun lying on the table, and the landlord stretched out on his back in the doorway with blood pumping from his groin. For James Pearce the day which had begun just like any other had ended in a nightmare from which there would be no awakening.

The trial of James Pearce for the wilful murder of James Hellard of the Rock House Inn began at the Somerset Summer Assizes at Wells on 15 August 1814 before Sir Vicary Gibbs.

Witnesses described the dispute over the payment for the cider, the scuffles in the bar and the intoxicated state of the prisoner. A witness by name of Parsons stated that earlier in the day he had been scaring and shooting birds with James Hellard's gun. On his return he had placed it loaded, but uncocked, in its usual place over the mantle piece in the bar and some six feet up the wall. He had been in the kitchen when he heard the shot and running to the bar found the landlord lying on the floor. The witness saw Pearce sitting at the far end of the bar and accused him of shooting James Hellard with a pistol but the prisoner had pointed to the gun lying on the table and claimed that it had gone off when he took it down from the wall. Parson's evidence was backed by another witness who had followed him into the bar.

In his defence James Pearce could give no reason why he took the gun down but it is most likely that because of his drink-fuddled state he could not remember. Neither did he argue that the gun might have been put up on the wall at full cock but suggested that it had been improperly let down to half cock and might possibly have gone off at the half cock when he took it down over the mantle piece. However, when the gun was brought into the court neither the judge nor members of the jury could fire it from the half cock position and no one tried it from the full cock to find out whether it could be discharged if accidentally knocked against the wall or mantlepiece of the bar.

Despite witnesses coming forward to tell of the prisoner's excellent character and every effort to prove that the gun had been fired accidentally, the jury found James Pearce guilty of the murder of James Hellard and with the judge and many in the crowded court in tears, he was sentenced to death.

The trial was not without incident when one of the witnesses was found to be drunk and the judge committed him into custody for contempt of court. It was also reported that despite the sympathy for James Pearce he appeared to be unconcerned for his fate and during much of the proceedings picked at an orange.

On the day before he was due to hang at Ilchester Gaol he penned the following letter to his parents in Frome:

Ilchester, Sunday, August 21st 1814

Having it impressed upon my mind to leave a declaration behind me, and now knowing I am to suffer death to-morrow morning for the wilful murder of Js. Hellard, I here solemnly in the presence of the God before whom I must shortly stand, declare that I never had the most distant thought ever to commit so horrid a deed, and I did not know, nor had no thought that the gun was loaded at the time it went off; it went off in my left hand entirely by accident: the gun was not cocked by me, but it is my firm belief the gun was put up cocked. I did not see the gun till the moment I took it down; and then I did not see the deceased, nor had I any thought of his coming, but I cannot say that I was entirely free from animosity, because I thought myself ill-used, but I had not formed any design to do him any personal injury whatsoever. I never told the witness Parsons, that 'I shot him with the gun,' and said 'there it is on the table,' nor that 'I took the gun down with my left hand and discharged it with my left hand:' I told him that it was not done with the pistol: it was the gun done it; and told him that I took the gun down with my left hand, and it went off in my left hand. But I forgive all my enemies, and die in charity with all mankind – not without hope that God of his infinite mercy will forgive me.

James Pearse

Without doubt the shooting of James Hellard was a terrible accident and although there had been a dispute over the payment for the cider, there was nothing in the evidence to prove a malicious or deliberate act on the part of James Pearce, or the reason for taking the gun down from the wall. It is also most likely that the witness Parsons put the gun back on the wall fully cocked by mistake but would not admit it for fear of being implicated in the death of the landlord of the Rock House Inn. Even now, nearly two centuries later, it is difficult to understand why a verdict of manslaughter was not returned but the jury decided that murder had been committed and that the accused must die was the only penalty for such a verdict.

THE SOUTH SOMERSET BREAD RIOTS

There was anger in the towns and villages of South Somerset in November 1867: food prices were very high, and in particular bread was now costing eightpence for a modest one pound loaf. Agricultural labourers at the time would be lucky to receive wages of ten shillings a week and a skilled factory worker could not expect more than £1. The eightpenny loaf was causing problems to hundreds of poor families throughout the area.

People blamed the local bakers for putting up the prices and the anger finally exploded in Chard on the evening of Monday, 11 November. Men, women and children began to assemble in the town centre and by seven o'clock there were several hundred people shouting and cheering. The crowd then marched to Mr Gawler's baker's shop in the High Street and, spurred on by a small number of troublemakers, stones were thrown breaking most of the windows of the property. Following the destruction of Mr Gawler's windows the mob's attention was turned to Mr Dyer's shop at the top of the town and all his windows shared the same fate.

During the disturbance, which was rapidly turning into a riot, the Town Council were meeting in emergency session and as the crowd passed the Town Hall on their way to attack the bakers in Fore Street, the mayor, Mr W. Salter, shouted from the balcony that what they were doing was illegal and useless and they should all go home. The mayor's exhortations may well have saved the day because it was reported that little damage was caused to the remaining bakers' shops and by midnight the streets of Chard were empty. During the disturbance the town police force – two constables – was powerless to intervene.

The following day the mayor issued handbills stating that the price of a loaf in Chard, at sevenpence, was cheaper than in the neighbouring towns of Taunton, Ilminster and Crewkerne, but no further reduction could be expected. Townspeople were told to stay at home and nearly all the tradesmen, together with many private residents, were sworn in as special constables. Police reinforcements arrived in Chard during the day and by Tuesday evening nearly forty police officers, supported by the specials, patrolled the town. A large crowd, however, defying the mayor's instructions, assembled once again in the High Street but on this occasion no disturbance took place and by midnight all was quiet. The police left early on Wednesday morning and the specials were stood down.

It was reported that most of the Monday stone-throwing had been carried out by women and boys 'invited doubtless by a few blackguards of the lowest order. The respectable working classes kept studiously aloof from such a senseless and useless attack upon property.'

The news of Monday's turmoil in Chard soon spread across South Somerset and on Tuesday evening some fifty 'big boys and girls' assembled in the Market Square at Ilminster and began chanting, 'We want a cheap loaf', 'Down with the tommy'(the police) and 'Chase the bobby'. A large crowd of several hundred people was soon drawn to the Square and it was reported that women considerably outnumbered the menfolk. One of the women was 'got up for the occasion, her hair was tied up in knots, her arms were bare, her frock pinned up, and not being very refined in her language she resembled "Meg Merrilees" in appearance.'

There were only two police constables on duty in Ilminster to face the crowd, and there was no hope of immediate reinforcement as the town force of an inspector, a sergeant and ten constables had been sent to Chard.

After much shouting, cheering and singing, a few stones were thrown at a butcher's shop and then the crowd divided in two 'in order to baffle the police.' One half marched down Ditton Street to the shop of Mr Walbridge, the first baker to increase the price of his loaves, and smashed over forty panes of glass to the shouts of 'Who rised the bread'and 'Short weight'. When Ilminster's two guardians of the law appeared on the scene, the crowd ran off.

In the meantime the second half of the crowd had turned their attention on the shop of Mrs Jacobs where they broke six panes of glass and a door panel. The shops of Mr Dawe and Mr Hickman were next in line but the appearance of the two intrepid constables dispersed the mob before it could do much damage.

The two parts of the crowd re-united and, pursued by the policemen, returned to the Market Square, where after more shouting and cheering, everyone went home. There was no further trouble in Ilminster during the rest of the week.

On Tuesday evening in Castle Cary, where the cost of bread was very high, the local police sergeant, assisted by officers from the neighbouring parishes, prevented trouble but during the following Wednesday evening a mob of several hundred paraded the streets. Although threats were shouted, there was no damage to property and, after the price of bread was reduced to eightpence on Thursday, everything remained quiet.

It was Yeovil's turn on Wednesday, 13 November when in the evening a large crowd assembled in the Borough and demands were shouted for bread prices to be reduced from eightpence per loaf. The appearance of the local police sergeant and several constables calmed passions but as the crowd went to their homes there were shouts of 'We'll be back tomorrow night.'

Thus warned, a small army of special constables was sworn in by the magistrates and when the crowd re-assembled on the Thursday evening it was overawed by the presence of the local police superintendent and his officers supported by the large body of specials. The crowd dispersed peacefully and Yeovil remained quiet during the succeeding days; even Fair night on the following Monday lacked its usual quota of 'disorderly characters.'

A serious situation, however, arose in South Petherton on Thursday, 14 November when, what was described as a large mob of about three hundred people, some armed with bludgeons and stone hammers, assembled at Pitney during the early evening and began to smash the bakers' shop windows as they moved through the town towards the Bell Inn. Here the mob was met by Sergeant Ashman supported by four constables who ordered them to disperse. The command was ignored and brandishing their bludgeons and other weapons in the sergeant's face the ringleaders defied him to read the Riot Act. The mob surged on smashing Mr Banfield's windows and, passing through South Street, destroyed the windows of Mr Ashman. In West Street they broke Mr Taylor's windows and then attacked the police officers and Mr Peren, a local solicitor, who two months later was still suffering from his injuries.

A full scale riot was now in progress and more shops and houses were attacked and damaged. The mob then set out to smash up Mr Banfield's mill but he, with considerable presence of mind, saved his property by liberally supplying the rioters with bread and cheese and cider as a reward for not doing so!

Rioting continued for over three hours during which time the magistrates managed to assemble a force of forty special constables who were armed with batons. Thus armed and led by the local police, the specials went into action against the mob and peace was soon restored for 'the roughs were unwilling to cross sticks with them.' The ringleaders of the riot were quickly taken into custody and there was no further trouble in South Petherton.

A riot was feared in Crewkerne on Friday, 15 November but the presence of large numbers of policemen resulted in a quiet evening.

On Monday, 18 November, a crowd of women assembled in the centre of Bruton and although there was a great deal of shouting and cheering there was no rioting or damage.

The last flare up occurred in Stoke-sub-Hamdon on Wednesday, 20 November, when a mob of youths started throwing stones at the doors of the village baker and then set off to Montacute, led by a lad blowing a horn. At Montacute, the mob failed to gain any recruits and after making a lot of noise they went home. There was no further trouble in the towns and villages of South Somerset and once again law and order returned: the poor gritted their teeth and struggled on.

Twenty South Petherton men and boys 'of the labouring classes' were brought before the Somerset Quarter Sessions in January 1868 charged with riot and assault and all but one, pleaded not guilty. Nineteen defendants were found guilty and sentenced to terms of imprisonment of between one and six months hard labour – one was acquitted.

A PROPHECY OF DISASTER

Our story starts in Yorkshire over four hundred years ago when, in a cave near the town of Knaresborough, a prophetess known as Mother Shipton, predicted that, on Good Friday in the year 1879, Ham Hill would be swallowed up in a great earthquake and Yeovil swept away in a great flood.

Rumours of these disastrous events began to circulate some six weeks before Easter 1879, and there were reports of people leaving their homes for safer parts, removing household goods from shelves and cupboards to prevent them being smashed in the impending earthquake, and delaying planting crops in their gardens. Ladies of a nervous disposition could be helped through the crisis by taking Kearsley's Widow Welches Female Pills whose 'wonderful efficacy' was claimed to be 'a most effective remedy for nervous depression.'

The excitement was apparently too much for James Palmer of Martock who, charged with being drunk and incapable on the evening of 4 April, told the magistrates that it was not alcohol but opium that had brought about his condition. The plea was accepted and James Palmer was discharged.

On Good Friday morning, 11 April, the intrepid correspondent of a local newspaper ventured to Ham Hill to report the disaster first hand before, presumably, being swallowed into the bowels of the earth. As he travelled to Stoke sub Hamdon he heard rumours that the great hill had already sunk by up to twelve feet and that houses in the vicinity had disappeared leaving only their chimney pots showing above ground. However, when he reached the stricken village he was no doubt relieved, and perhaps not a little disappointed, to find no evidence of the feared catastrophe. Indeed, the first person the correspondent met, said that he was on his way to work at the Ham Hill quarries with no worries at all and it would take a lot to knock the old hill down. The quarryman confirmed that Mother Shipton's prophecy had been taken seriously by some of the local people, but as far as he was concerned, he had planted his potatoes and they were growing well.

When the correspondent reached the top of Ham Hill, somewhat breathless after the steep climb, he found business as usual in the quarries. Everyone he spoke to told him that although many people had been frightened by the prediction it had not worried them. 'The person who put it about ought to be shot,' they told him. The correspondent observed loftily that 'it was evident that a strong belief existed in a portion of the lower classes in the parish that the thing might occur but they were disinclined to admit they were superstitious.'

The day passed uneventfully, to the great relief of many people. 'But some of them will remember Good Friday 1879 for as long as they live,' the correspondent concluded.

THE SHOOTING OF LORD GLASTONBURY'S GAMEKEEPER

It was early in the evening of 3 July 1823, when Thomas Pearce, one of Lord Glastonbury's gamekeepers, heard a gunshot as he rode his horse down a lane near land rented by the Voke family at Compton Dundon. Dismounting, he walked across a couple of fields and his suspicions were confirmed when he came upon young Samuel Voke reloading his gun. Although the Vokes rented this field from the Glastonbury Estate, the shooting rights were not included, and Thomas Pearce had long suspected Samuel of hunting game on the land; he had now caught him red-handed.

The keeper told young Voke that he was poaching and as this was a serious offence he would have to report him. Samuel begged to be pardoned but Pearce replied that that was not within his power. However Mr Ryall, the estate steward, might be prepared to let him off the charge and Samuel Voke agreed to go with the keeper to the steward's house.

The two men walked side by side back across the fields but just before they reached the lane Thomas Pearce went on ahead to fetch his horse. Suddenly there was a bang from behind, and the keeper felt a blow like a kick from a horse: Samuel Voke had fired his gun into the man's back and then made off.

Thomas Pearce was a very lucky man because his thick loose clothes absorbed most of the shot. However, some of the pellets peppered his back and he was severely bruised. Thinking his back broken, Thomas Pearce did not pursue the attacker and after mounting his horse with much difficulty began to make a slow way home. The injured man had gone no more than half a mile when suddenly his horse shied as a figure appeared from behind a large ash tree less than four yards away on the right of the lane. Thomas Pearce had time to recognise Samuel Voke and to look down the barrel of his gun before it went off blasting away the gamekeeper's right eye, seven teeth and parts of his cheek and neck. Miraculously, the sixty-six-year-old man was not fatally wounded and managed to retain his seat and ride the mile and a half to the steward's residence. Mr Ryall helped the wounded keeper from his horse and after applying poultices to the wounds, sent for a surgeon. For several days Thomas Pearce's life hung in the balance, but he was a strong man for his age, and made a slow recovery.

The search was now on for Samuel Voke who had fled from Compton Dundon, and within a few days he was arrested at Hallatrow, near Midsomer Norton. He appeared at the Bridgwater Assizes in August, charged with the capital offence of maliciously and wilfully shooting at Thomas Pearce with intent to murder him. The trial was short, the prisoner found guilty and sentenced to death.

During the time Samuel Voke spent awaiting his fate at Ilchester Gaol he was said to have been truly repentant and on the eve of his execution Thomas Pearce visited the condemned man and they were reconciled. At eleven o'clock on the morning of 26 November 1823 Samuel Voke ascended the platform of the gallows and after praying with the prison chaplain for some fifteen minutes, the rope was fastened around his neck, the white cap drawn down over his face and the trap fell away.

Samuel Voke was described as being a remarkably fine young man, twenty-one years of age and the son of respectable parents who occupied a small farm at Compton Dundon.

BAD BLOOD IN
LEIGH-ON-MENDIP

T he peaceful aspect of a village can quite often mask undercurrents of conflict and tangled relationships. Usually they remain hidden beneath the tranquil surface, but occasionally they erupt, and no more spectacularly than in the village of Leigh-on-Mendip in the autumn of 1857.

Sunday evening, 27 September, was dark and wet, and the lamps were lit early in the parish church of St Giles for divine service. The curate, the Reverend George Augustus Mahon, was nearing the end of his sermon and many of his congregation were no doubt dozing or beginning to think of supper, when there was a tremendous crash! For a moment there was silence, and then pandemonium. Women screamed, children cried, and the congregation stared in horror as Mr Mahon slumped semi-conscious in his pulpit, covered in blood while smoke drifted up to the roof above the north aisle. While some worshippers fled in panic or milled about, others gathered their wits and rushed forward to help the curate down from the blood-spattered pulpit. It was quickly established that apart from bruising to his forehead and an injury to his right eye, the clergyman was not seriously hurt and the blood was not his. A hole in one of the windows of the north wall and a spray of blood across the church to the pulpit, revealed that someone had fired a gun loaded with gore at the curate. Although several men rushed out into the churchyard the culprit had disappeared into the wet autumn night.

To the shocked clergyman, there was one prime suspect and that was Joseph Ashman, a well known local farmer, whose conduct towards the curate had resulted in his eviction from the farm he had leased from the rector.

Joseph Ashman was found in company with Henry Plaister and James Turner at the Tadhill Inn about a mile from the village and, on the curate's instruction, all three were arrested by the local police constable and taken in custody to Frome. Plaister and Turner were quickly released but Joseph Ashman was brought before the Frome magistrates charged with having discharged a gun loaded with blood at the Reverend George Augustus Mahon during divine service on 27 September. However, despite two appearances before the magistrates, and considerable police activity, including investigations by a detective brought down from London, the evidence obtained could not sustain the prosecution. In the close-knit community of Leigh-on-Mendip, witnesses were reluctant to come forward and those who did were unsatisfactory. No one would swear that they had seen Joseph Ashman fire the gun, the weapon had not been recovered, and after thirteen days in Shepton Mallet gaol he was released – no case to answer. It seemed that the shooting would remain an unsolved crime, the close relationships in the village preventing anyone 'telling tales'. A particularly nasty and stupid piece of vandalism occurred in the village on the following 5 November, Guy Fawkes night, when someone shot out and completely destroyed the principal stained glass window of St Giles Church. The *Somerset & Wilts Journal* of 14 November was outraged, and recalled that this form of 'barbarism' had not been uncommon in the parish some fifty years before.

Six months later the case of the shooting of Mr Mahon was reopened when two frightened witnesses came forward to testify against Joseph Ashman and he was arrested. This time the evidence was sufficient for the magistrates to send him for trial at the forthcoming Somerset Assizes and the two witnesses were given protection.

Joseph Ashman appeared before Mr Justice Crowder at the Assizes in Taunton on Monday, 29 March 1858, and pleaded not guilty to feloniously firing at the Reverend George Augustus Mahon, at Leigh-on-Mendip, on 27 September last with a gun loaded with gunpowder and blood, with intent to do him some grievous bodily harm. Mr Prideaux and Mr Kerslake prosecuted and Mr Edwards and Mr Thring defended.

After outlining the prosecution's case Mr Prideaux called his first witness, the Reverend George Mahon who stated that towards the close of his sermon at about 7.15pm, a gun had been fired at him from the third window of the north aisle. The charge had struck him on the right forehead and he had fallen stunned in the steps of the pulpit. On recovering his senses, he found that his white surplice was covered in blood, there was blood on the Bible and on some of the congregation. The church was in uproar but after he had managed to quieten everyone, he was helped to the vestry where his bloodstained garments were removed and a piece of glass taken from his right eye.

The witness recalled that he had gone home and was there told that Joseph Ashman had recently bought some blood from the village butcher, and a gun seen earlier in the day in a room which the prisoner used was no longer there. Police Constable Alfred Urch, the village policeman, was called, and they went to the Tadhill Inn where they found Joseph Ashman, in company with Henry Plaister and

James Turner, and the three men were taken into custody on suspicion of the shooting. Mr Mahon recalled that although he had been well enough to walk to the Tadhill Inn on the night of the shooting, the effect of the blow had caused giddiness and great weakness from which he still suffered.

Cross-examined, the witness stated that since coming into the curacy of the parish about three and a half years before, he had made no alterations except, finding a prevalence of heavy drinking, had gone to the public house and spoken to the drunkards as they came out. He had complained to the Reverend Mr Horner, the rector of Mells and lord of the manor, who owned most of the parish including the farm occupied by Joseph Ashman, about the prisoner's conduct. The curate had told the rector that the prisoner beat his wife and was a drunkard, and had, in a village revel, led a man dressed as a woman through the village to the clergyman's house. He stated that the prisoner had often muttered words against religion and he had taken note every time the prisoner had muttered 'damn' as he passed by. There had been occasions when Joseph Ashman had been up a ladder and when he saw the curate he would shout out, 'I'm going up Jacob's ladder!' Mr Mahon stated that the prisoner was a man of considerable importance in the village and this was why he had felt it necessary to speak of his conduct to the rector. It was because of this that Joseph Ashman had been evicted from his farm. George Terry, surgeon of Mells, stated that he had attended Mr Mahon about an hour after the shooting and found the right side of his forehead highly inflamed and had had to remove from it grains of gunpowder. The curate's eye was also injured and he had been in a very shocked state.

The next witness, Martha Oleronshaw, testified that on the Sunday evening at about a quarter to seven the prisoner had passed her house going in the direction of the church which was a walk of about three or four minutes.

Walter Shepherd stated that he had seen Joseph Ashman go into Mark Ashmans's house opposite the church with a gun on the Saturday afternoon and Henry Heard testified to seeing a gun in a room in that house on the Sunday morning. He had been in church when the shot had been fired and had immediately gone to Mark Ashman's house and found the gun missing. The reason he had done this was not revealed at the trial. Cross-examined, the witness agreed that the room where he had seen the gun was used by all Mark Ashman's family. John Oleronshaw testified that Joseph Ashman had owned two guns and was a good shot.

The evidence of the next two witnesses was the most crucial to the prosecution and held up under intense cross-examination and ridicule at the magistrates' hearing.

John Hiscox, a twenty-year-old labourer, was the first to enter the witness box and recalled that on the Sunday evening he had walked from the hamlet of Soho to Leigh-on-Mendip with Elizabeth Plaister and leaving her in the main street, he had gone into the church porch to wait for his brother who was at the service. He heard someone come through the church gate and in the light of the porch lamp he saw Joseph Ashman walking up the path. Ashman had then turned left and walked across to the wall on the west side of the churchyard. The witness stated that it was most unusual for anyone to walk around the church on a dark wet evening because there was no path and nowhere to go. He had therefore followed the prisoner and saw him go along beside the wall and out through a little door into the 'drang', or pathway, on the opposite side of which was the timber yard owned by Thomas Ashman, the prisoner's brother. Joseph Ashman returned a few moments later with a gun, walked to the end window of the north aisle and fired into the church; he had then run back out of the churchyard through the door in the wall. The witness stated that he had been so frightened he had run out into the street and told no one what he had seen. However, on 20 March last, the curate had asked him if he knew anything about the shooting and he had told him everything. John Hiscox stated that he hadn't said anything before because he was afraid that the prisoner would 'do him an accident.'

Under intense cross-examination, the witness refused to change his testimony. He denied telling several people that he had been falling asleep in the church porch and had been woken up by the sound of the shot and had seen no one.

Sixteen-year-old labourer Matthew Lane, now entered the witness box. He recalled that at about twenty-to-seven on the Sunday evening he had left Mr Cosh's farm where he worked, and had gone up the lane by the church into a field where he had relieved himself. Suddenly a shot rang out from the direction of the church and moments later he saw the prisoner running up the lane and climb over the stile into the field where he was standing by the hedge. Matthew Lane stated that Joseph Ashman had passed within about four yards and although it was quite dark, he could see that he was carrying a gun in his left hand with the butt pointing forwards. The prisoner then climbed over the wall of his brother's timber yard and disappeared.

The witness said that he had been very frightened and had run down the path as fast as he could. He recalled that about a week after the shooting a boy called Thomas Ashman, of Stoke Lane, a relative of the prisoner, had shown him a gun hidden in some hoops beside the boiler of the engine in Mr Thomas Ashman's timber shed, and said that this was the 'gun that the blood was put in.' He had held the gun and noticed some bloody fingerprints on the stock. The witness had been too frightened to tell anyone until he heard that John Hiscox had made a statement. Matthew Lane had then told his master, Mr Cosh, but after giving his evidence to the magistrates he had been fearful of going home. He had therefore spent a day and night with Mr Oleronshaw, the next with Mr Mahon, and then at a house in Frome before coming to Taunton where he lodged at the Squirrel Inn.

Police constable Alfred Urch stated that he had been called to the church following the shooting but although he had immediately searched the churchyard and adjoining fields he had found nothing. Following information given to him by Mr Mahon, he had gone in company with the curate to the Tadhill Inn and arrested Joseph Ashman on suspicion of shooting blood. The prisoner had denied the charge and although he admitted that he had purchased some blood from Butcher Ellery he claimed that this had been used for mixing cattle medicine. The constable stated that he had found no blood when he searched the prisoner's room in Mark Ashman's house.

The prosecution's case was now complete and defence counsel, Mr Edwards rose and addressed the jury. He naturally deplored what had happened at the service but he believed that whoever had fired the gun had no intention of inflicting grievous bodily harm on Mr Mahon. At the moment there were two parties in the Church of England; one group of clergymen who chose to preach in a black gown and another preferring a white surplice – Mr Mahon had chosen the latter. In view of the strong feelings which this could arouse, he suggested that the man who had fired the gun did so for no other purpose that that of sprinkling the parson's white surplice with blood. Mr Edwards believed that the prisoner was entirely innocent and he suggested that the actions of the Reverend Mahon were motivated by malice. He thought that a clergyman's duty was to live in peace and charity with all mankind, and if he found any one of his parishioners to be guilty of improper conduct he should speak to him like a brother and seek to mend his ways. The actions of the prisoner may have been foolish, but a man dressed as a woman, as at the village revel, was not unusual in Europe during a carnival, and was not of sufficient gravity to seek the prisoner's eviction from his farm.

Mr Edwards then called Betty Padfield who stated that she had been walking past the church gate when she had heard a shot and saw John Hiscox run out of the porch and down the path towards her. She had asked him what had happened and whether he had seen anyone but he had said no because he had been dropping off to sleep when the shot had woken him up. Several other witnesses then testified that John Hiscox had told them a similar story.

Blacksmith John Lane, the brother of witness Matthew Lane, stated that his brother had been at home at the time the shot was fired but denied threatening to cut his heart out if he gave evidence against the prisoner. Mr Mahon was recalled and testified that John Lane had stood outside his house and shouted out, 'Mat! Mat! come on out; I'll cut your damned heart out if you don't!' The boy, Thomas Ashman, denied finding the gun in the timber shed and telling Matthew Lane that the blood had been fired from it. Joseph Ashman, stated that he had care of the engine and machinery in Mr Thomas Ashman's timber yard and he had never seen a gun beside the boiler.

Jane Lane, Matthew's mother, testified that her son had been at home asleep on the Sunday evening and the first she had known of the shooting was when her husband came home from chapel and told her that someone had shot the parson with blood. She had sent Matthew to his master, Mr Cosh, to find out if it were true. Cross-examined, Jane Lane denied threatening to break her son's head if he gave evidence against Joseph Ashman. However Emma Cosh and her daughter Mary were called and testified that Matthew had been reading at their house on the Sunday evening and had left at about twenty to seven.

George Ellery, the village butcher, recalled drinking with the prisoner at the Tadhill Inn on the Sunday evening and as they left he heard the clock strike seven. The two men had walked towards Stoke St Michael for about ten minutes but then Joseph Ashman had decided to return for some more beer. The witness stated that the prisoner could not walk very well because some years before he had broken both his legs. Constable Urch was recalled and stated that George Ellery had told him the day after the shooting that he had left Joseph Ashman at the Tadhill Inn.

A character witness, grocer Henry Season, spoke well of the prisoner and said that he was a good neighbour.

The case was now closed and Mr Justice Crowder summed up. After reviewing the evidence he stated that the question was not whether grievous bodily harm was done, but whether grievous bodily harm was intended. If the jury thought that harm was intended then they must consider whether the prisoner was the person who fired the gun.

After some deliberation the jury decided that the prisoner had fired the gun but found him not guilty of intent to do grievous bodily harm. The judge stated that this was in effect a verdict of not guilty on this charge. However, Joseph Ashman was kept in custody to be tried the next day on another charge.

The second trial began at nine o'clock on the following morning before Mr Justice Willes and a new jury was sworn in.

On this occasion Joseph Ashman was indicted for unlawfully inflicting bodily harm on the Reverend George Augustus Mahon, and to this he pleaded not guilty. The trial was a repeat of the previous day's but this time the jury found the prisoner guilty. In passing sentence, the judge strongly condemned the prisoner's actions and concurred with the verdict. He stated, however, that Mr Mahon had asked for mercy to be shown to the prisoner and because of this worthy and generous act he would pass the mild sentence of imprisonment for twelve calendar months.

There is a memorial brass on the north wall of St Giles' church near the window through which the shot was fired which reads:

To the memory
of
The Reverend George Augustus Mahon MA Oxon
for 41 years Curate in Charge and Vicar
of this parish.
Born October 23 1828
Died at New Clee Vicarage Grimsby August 6 1899
This brass is erected by the parishioners of Leigh-on-Mendip
in grateful remembrance of his long and faithful ministry

A SHORT STEP
AND A LONG DROP

It is amazing how often sensible people make most peculiar decisions – more often than not nothing serious happens but sometimes the decision may prove fatal. Take, for example, the case of the commercial traveller's strange decision made on a Monday evening in late September 1901.

The evening train from Weymouth came to a stop at the home signal some two hundred yards from Yeovil Pen Mill station and waited for the Durston train to enter the station; it was 7.15pm and the branch train was over ten minutes late. The sixth carriage of the Weymouth train was standing on the bridge which crosses the stream from the weir pool below Wyndham Hill and, in one of the compartments, Mr Henry Edginton of Weston-super-Mare, a commercial traveller for Booths Distillery Company, was dozing after a hard days selling. Mr Edginton's fellow passengers in the compartment, commercial representative Mr Tom Lewis, and Mr Percy Martin, the gardener at Hendford Manor, were somewhat surprised when he suddenly stood up and opened the carriage door. Mr Lewis shouted a warning that the train was not yet in the station but, to his dismay, after retorting, 'I know Yeovil better than you do!' Mr Edginton stepped out into the gathering darkness, on to the parapet of the bridge and dropped 25 feet into the stream below. The two passengers left in the compartment looked at each other in horror and on hearing a loud splash Mr Lewis exclaimed, 'He's done for!' At that moment the train moved forward and into Pen Mill station. On being told of the incident, the district inspector based at the station, Mr Alfred Daniels, grabbed a hand lamp and followed by the station master, lineman Woodley and a passenger, set out along the track to the bridge. Clambering down the embankment they found Mr Edginton lying on the large stones in the shallow stream groaning and muttering, 'Where am I?' and, 'I wonder what brought me here?' Nearby was his silk top hat floating in the stream, undamaged. The commercial traveller was a very big man weighing nearly sixteen stone and it took some time to drag him from the stream and up the embankment to the railway track. A stretcher was sent for and the gravely injured man was carried back to the station. Here Mr Edginton was placed in a compartment of the eight o'clock Durston branch train and conveyed to Yeovil Town Station from which he was taken by horse bus to hospital. At about 8.30pm Doctor Kingston arrived at the hospital and examined the patient whom he described as a large, well-developed man, wet through, and suffering from very severe shock, a large jagged cut on the back of his head and a frac- ture of the left shoulder. Despite all his efforts, Dr Kingston could not save the unfortunate Mr Edginton who died some forty minutes later.

The inquest was held in the Victoria Hall and after hearing the reports and evidence from the witnesses, the coroner concluded that the deceased Mr Edginton knew Yeovil well, he had not appeared to be under the influence of drink and that his motives for getting out on the bridge were entirely speculative for, as he commented, 'There must have been a strong motive passing through the deceased's mind to get out at this place where he thought he could safely alight and felt it his bounden duty to do so.'

The jury returned a verdict of death from misadventure, and the late Mr Edginton was taken home to Weston-super-Mare.

THE ERRAND BOY'S COURAGE

It was very cold and frosty in the week leading up to Christmas in 1901 and all across the country people were enjoying happy hours skating on ice-covered ponds and lakes.

Chard was no exception and on Sunday afternoon, 22 December, Mrs Sarah Melhuish, of Furnham Road, took her young son and his friend, Eric James, for a walk to see the ice on the frozen reservoir. A small crowd had gathered in the Chaffcombe Road to look at a motor car parked on the bridge over the Taunton and Chard branch railway line and, being curious, Sarah went to see this fairly rare sight; in the meantime the two young boys ran down to the nearby reservoir. Suddenly her son was pulling at her skirts shouting that Eric had fallen through the ice and, running to the shore, Sarah was horrified to see the lad struggling in the deep freezing water.

The frozen Chard reservoir had been a popular skating rink for many years and amongst the youngsters enjoying themselves on the ice was a fifteen-year-old errand boy, Lawrence Hussey, of Greenhill, Furnham Road. Seeing Eric fall through the ice, Lawrence skated to the rescue and as he neared the jagged hole he lay down and eased himself towards the struggling boy. At the edge Lawrence reached out to the youngster but as he did so the ice gave way and now he was fighting for life in the freezing reservoir.

An off-duty Great Western Railway fireman, Alfred Pearce, was enjoying a quiet stroll and watching the skaters when he heard the cries for help and, going on to the ice, he began to edge forward towards the hole where Lawrence was struggling to keep Eric afloat. Now Alfred Pearce was also in great danger as the ice was cracking all around him but he kept going only to witness the two lads, overcome by cold, sink slowly out of sight just as he reached them. The gallant fireman managed to return to the shore before the ice completely broke under him.

The police were called and Sergeant Attwood, accompanied by Constable Phillips, were soon on the scene but during the hours which followed all efforts to recover the bodies with ladders and ropes failed. A sunken boat lying in the northern end of the reservoir was raised and brought down the Chaffcombe Road to the spot but when it was launched it leaked so badly that it was considered too dangerous to use.

George Warner, a marine engineer, of Victoria Avenue, had now joined the recovery party and organised the construction of a large raft from ladders, wooden farm gates and barrels. At about ten o'clock that evening, George Warner and Fred Symes launched the raft and after a fifteen minutes search with a grappling line the two men brought Lawrence Hussey's body to the surface; it took another hour to locate and recover the small corpse of Eric James.

In memory of this selfless act, a drinking trough was bought by the people of Chard for the thirsty horses of the town and this can still be seen at Millfield. It bears the following inscription:

This Drinking trough was erected by the inhabitants
of CHARD in remembrance of a brave deed bravely done
on 22nd December, 1901 when Lawrence Hussey aged 15
lost his life in an attempt to save Eric James, a drowning
boy, at the reservoir near this town.

THE MURDER OF INNOCENTS

The tragic deaths of new-born children featured large in the coroners' courts of Victorian England. Many were the result of neglect from the poverty or ignorance of the parents, some were accidental and others were the result of undiagnosed illnesses. Some, however, were more sinister. Another mouth to feed in grinding poverty, an unwanted baby, a bastard child, the fear of the workhouse and terrible despair could result in the murder of innocents.

A little after nine o'clock on the morning of 23 January 1857, thirteen-year-old James Lanham was on his way to work when he saw a brown paper parcel half hidden in the roadside ditch near Goar Knap in Yeovil. James retrieved the parcel and as he opened it something wrapped in a dirty cloth fell out. His curiosity aroused, the boy unravelled the bundle and to his horror he found the bloody body of a baby.

Police Superintendent Holt was called to the scene and the pathetic bundle was taken to the White Horse, a nearby beer house, where a post-mortem examination was performed by Mr W.F. Tomkyns, a local surgeon.

The inquest was held in the Pen Mill Hotel and in his evidence, Mr Tomkyns told the jury that the body was that of a newborn well-formed healthy female child who had lived for several hours before being fatally battered about the head. He believed that the child had been dead for at least a week.

Despite extensive police inquiries in the area no one had been arrested on suspicion of causing the baby's death and the inquest jury returned a verdict of 'murder by some person or persons but by whom there was no evidence to show.' The killer of the baby in the bundle was never discovered.

Twelve years later, the body of a child was discovered in Yeovil in bizarre and gruesome circumstances. Early in June, 1869, Henry Carpenter and Thomas Millard were draining the reservoir of a disused gasometer at the town gasworks when to their horror they discovered the decomposing body of a child, minus an arm.

The police were called and the bloated corpse was lodged in the stables of the Elephant and Castle public house to await the post-mortem examination. At the inquest it was suggested that the body had been pushed down into the narrow space between the gasometer and the wall of the reservoir where there would be small chance of its discovery. It had been impossible to establish the cause of death or sex of the child or indeed how long it had been in the reservoir, as the tar- and gas-saturated water had acted as a preservative.

The jury returned a verdict of 'found dead' and the pathetic corpse was buried in Division B, plot 1216, at Yeovil cemetery on 11 June 1869.

On Sunday, 23 January, 1870, Emily Tuttiett and John Larcombe drew some water from the well in Long Acre Lane in Somerton but recoiled in disgust at the mess floating in the bucket. Closer examination revealed a piece of flesh and looking down the well, John Larcombe could just make out an object floating in the water. The bucket was let down again and after a few minutes the object was captured and drawn up. It was the decomposed body of a child wrapped in a sodden rag.

The inquest was held in the Crown Inn and evidence was given by Emily Tuttiett and John Larcombe, the latter commenting that for some time before the discovery of the body, he had felt ill after drinking water from the well. The post-mortem was carried out by Mr Clement Edkins, a Somerton surgeon, who stated that although the body was very decomposed he could establish that it was that of a healthy female infant, born alive and whose throat had been cut. The police had no suspect but told the inquest that they were vigorously pursuing their inquiries. A verdict of 'wilful murder against some person or persons unknown' was returned but despite a reward of £50 the culprit was never brought to justice.

Five months later in May 1870, John White found a child's body floating in the mill pond at Bruton. Dr Higginbotham, who carried out the post-mortem told the inquest that the child's skull had been fractured in three places and he did not believe this could have been caused accidentally. However the doctor could not confirm that the child 'had a separate existence.' Despite the strong suspicion that the child had been murdered the jury returned an open verdict of 'being found dead in the mill pond' and so it was to remain.

Although many of the cases of violent deaths of infants were never solved, some were and these caused sensations at the time.

Jane Willis, who was still unmarried at thirty-one lived with her eight-year-old daughter, Sarah Ann, her father, mother and brother, Edward, in the village of Queen Camel, near Yeovil, and in the autumn of 1857 the village was rife with gossip. Despite her constant denials, Jane Willis was obviously pregnant, and there were rumours that she had threatened to do away with the child when it was born. These threats would be recalled at the 1857 Winter Assizes at Taunton, when she stood trial before the Honourable Sir James Shaw Willes, charged with the wilful murder of her infant child.

The first witness called by the Crown was Mrs Mary Ann Shean who said that she had known for some time that Jane Willis was in the family way and she had offered to give some clothes for the child if the prisoner would own up. The witness went on to say that at about four o'clock on the afternoon of Friday, 30 October she had seen the prisoner come out of her house with something bundled up in her arms and walk towards the stream which ran along the bottom of the garden. Jane Willis had then noticed the witness watching her and had turned off through the hedge of her garden and gone into the communal privy. About five minutes later the prisoner had emerged without the bundle but when Mary Shean had accused her of drowning the baby she had been told to hush her voice. The witness went on to describe how she had called out to two of her neighbours, Mrs Edith Thorne and Mrs Mary Parsons, and the three women had gone into the Willis's house and demanded to examine Jane as they believed a child had been born and done away with. Despite the prisoner's denials and protests the women lifted her skirts and found the evidence they were looking for: Jane Willis had been delivered of a child. The three women then went to the privy and peering down through the holes spied a bundle floating in the muck. Mary Shean went on to tell how they had secured the object with a pair of old iron tongs but their efforts to lift it out had failed

Mary Shean's evidence was corroborated by her neigbours, Edith Thorne and Mary Parsons, when they followed her into the witness box.

Police Constable Alfred Everley recalled how he had gone to the prisoner's house but she had vehemently denied having borne a child. However on searching the house he had found blood marks leading from the stairs to the privy from which he retrieved a bundle of rags containing the dead body of a new-born infant. The constable had taken the body to Mr Jey, the local surgeon, and returned to the prisoner's house where he heard her daughter talking about a knife. When questioned the child had told him that her mother had come downstairs and picked up a knife which was now on the window sill of the bedroom. Constable Everley found the knife, which was broken and rusty with the end bent up, and took it to Mr Jey.

Cross-examined, Constable Everley admitted that he had found no blood on the knife and the points on the tongs which he and the women had used during their efforts to lift the bundle out of the privy were not sharp.

Sarah Ann Willis, the prisoner's eight-year-old daughter, remembered her mother coming down stairs, taking the knife and going back up again. After a while her mother had come down and had gone out into the garden carrying something in her apron. Sarah Ann could not see what she was holding but her mother did not have it when came back and there was blood on her apron. Her mother had then sat down and begun to peel potatoes.

The prisoner's brother, Edward Willis, testified that his sister had told him several months before 30 October that if it was her lot to have a child she would put it away and never have it alive. She had refused to name the father and even though she was obviously in the family way, continued to deny it. Willis disclosed that on the morning of 30 October, his mother had asked Jane when she was going to the Workhouse to have the baby and she had replied, 'Not this fortnight.' There were gasps from the court when the witness revealed that on the day before the child was born Jane had told her mother that she did not want any clothes as she would put it away.

Mr Charles Jey, the surgeon, took the stand and recalled that late in the afternoon of 30 October, Constable Everley had brought to his surgery the dead body of a new-born infant and explained the circumstances of its discovery. On examining the body he had found marks of violence and with Mr Latham, his assistant, he had gone to the prisoner's house. To begin with she had stoutly denied giving birth to a child but the surgeon's examination established beyond doubt that the prisoner had been recently confined. Mr Jey then described the post-mortem he had carried out a few days later with the assistance of Mr Wallace, a surgeon from Castle Cary, and Mr Latham. The body was a newborn, full-grown female child, weighing five and a half pounds, which in his opinion and that of his medical colleagues had been born alive. The surgeon now turned to the condition of the body and stated that he had found the right eye protruding from its socket and eleven wounds on the head, face, right ear and right neck; the rest of the body was free of injury. The wounds varied in severity from superficial cuts to deep incisions on the head and neck. A more detailed examination of the child's head revealed a fracture of the skull and a haemorrhage caused by one of the incisions. The blade of the knife found in the prisoner's room fitted the fracture wound. Mr Jey concluded his evidence by saying that in his opinion the wounds had been inflicted when the child was alive and were sufficient to have caused its death. Cross-examined the surgeon stated that he did not believe that the fracture to the child's skull could have been caused during a normal birth. Although there were cases when considerable force would have to be used he considered that a woman could not have produced such a fracture by delivering the child herself.

At this point the judge intervened and said that it appeared to him that it would be unsafe to convict the prisoner on the charge of murder, but there was the alternative charge of concealment of birth, about which there could hardly be any doubt. The law did not hold that injuries inflicted during delivery and before birth was actually complete, would sustain a charge of murder. He confessed there were a great many circumstances of suspicion in this case, but on the other hand there were some which seemed to diminish their effect, when considered with respect to the capital charge. The judge said that it seemed almost impossible that the knife which had been produced could have been used for the purpose of inflicting any injury upon the child because if it had the wounds would have been far more serious than those which had been described, and the fracture of the head might have been caused during delivery, or with the tongs which had been used to extricate the body from the privy. If the jury agreed with him they would probably consider that although this case was not free from suspicion, the safer course would be to return a verdict of which there could be no doubt and convict the prisoner of concealment of birth.

The trial now closed and the jury returned a verdict of not guilty to murder but guilty of concealment of birth and Jane Willis was sentenced to eighteen months hard labour.

The census of 1861 for Queen Camel shows that Jane Willis had returned to the village and was living with her now widowed mother, her daughter, Sarah Ann, sister Elizabeth and brother Edward and his wife Sophia. Two of the women who testified against Jane at her trial, Mary Ann Shean and Edith Thorne, still lived nearby.

THE QUACK DOCTOR FROM CREWKERNE

'I believed he was going to cure her but she got worse,' Mrs Emma Foot of Odcombe told the Yeovil Borough Magistrates on a Friday morning in June 1876.

Frederick Culliford of Crewkerne, described as a 'quack doctor' had been brought before the Court charged with obtaining three shillings from Emma Foot under false pretences.

Earlier Mrs Foot had explained that her mother, Jane Kimber, had been ill with a very bad arm and she believed this was caused by someone casting a spell on her. Having heard that a quack doctor called Frederick Culliford could break spells, she had gone into Yeovil and met him in a beerhouse in Middle Street. She had brought some of her mother's 'water' in a small bottle which she gave to Culliford after explaining her fears. On taking the bottle he shook it, examined the contents and confirmed that there was a spell on Emma's mother. The bottle was shaken again and then the 'quack' put some thorns into it followed by a piece of paper. He told Emma that an ill wish had been placed on her mother by a near neighbour who could be seen from the bedroom window of her house.

Culliford returned the bottle with instructions that it should be buried upside down in Mrs Kimber's garden and said that so long as it remained undisturbed she would get well. If she didn't Emma was to return in three weeks time and he would give her some medicinal powders for her mother. She handed over three shillings and returned home, placing the bottle in the garden as instructed.

Sadly Mrs Kimber did not get better, and when she was told that the condition of a sick woman in Preston Plucknett had not been improved by Frederick Culliford's services, Emma dug up the bottle and made a complaint to the Yeovil police.

At the hearing, Frederick Culliford's solicitor sought to prove that his client had not obtained the money by false pretences but had agreed to supply some medicinal powders and had done all that he could for the sick woman. These protestations did not satisfy Mrs Foot who exclaimed that if he could not do her mother any good 'he ought not to have taken the money from me. Mother was nearly dead and I wanted to know who was trying to kill her. He did more harm than good!'

The Mayor of Yeovil, who was chairman of the magistrates, then read out the charm which had been written on the paper put in the bottle.

As long as this paper remains in this bottle of water of mine, I hope Satan, that angel of darkness will pour out his wrath upon the person who has been privately injuring me for a long time past, and put them upon a bed of sickness with the most violent pains that ever man was troubled with for ever, and such as no man or woman living can cure; and as this water is fomented and troubled with these thorn prickles, so shall the flesh on their body be also fomented and troubled at the same time with the most violent pains for ever; and as this water do waste and dry away at the same time, until there is nothing left but the skin and bare bones, and they shall not live for more than 90 days from this day, and no longer; and then go to hell everlasting, there to dwell with the Devil and his angels until the terrible day of the Lord, and then be judged by the deeds done by them towards me when living upon earth.

Concluding the reading the mayor remarked that if this wasn't false pretences he didn't know what was! On being told that the case would be sent for trial at the next Quarter Sessions, Frederick Culliford stated that the money he had received 'from she, sir, was for my advice and that alone, which I always give. I never charge anything for any bottle.'

The Yeovil magistrates committed the defendant on two charges; first, for obtaining three shillings from Emma Foot by false pretences and second, for pretending to exercise or use some kind of influence of witchcraft under the Witchcraft Act of 1735. At the Quarter Sessions Frederick Culliford was found not guilty of the first charge but guilty of the second and sentenced to twelve month's imprisonment for the offence under the Witchcraft Act.

THE FALL OF A WYVERN

The Wyvern was a large single-engine strike fighter designed by Westland Aircraft of Yeovil to meet the Admiralty's specification for a large carrier/land-based fighter with the capacity to operate in an anti-shipping role. It was a machine of complex design and, in the autumn of 1949, was still in its development stage with all the dangers and difficulties this entailed. Monday morning, 31 October, was a crisp autumn day under a clear blue sky when Westland's assistant chief test pilot, Squadron Leader Mike Graves DFC, took the Wyvern prototype VP113, powered by a Python turboprop engine fitted with two contra-rotating propellers, up for a routine test flight from the company's airfield at Merryfield, near Ilminster. As it flew over Yeovil the aircraft developed engine trouble and Mike Graves made for an emergency landing at the Westland airfield.

The stricken Wyvern swooped low over the town and across the airfield, climbed over Preston Plucknett and banked left for a landing approach from the west when its engine stopped. The aircraft came in wheels up for a forced 'belly' landing at something like 200 mph but despite Mike Grave's efforts to reduce the speed it crossed the crown of the airfield before it touched down. The Wyvern bounced into the air, ploughed through the eastern perimeter fence killing five-year-old Ann Wilkins as she pedalled her tricycle along the cinder path to Seaton Road, smashed on across a piece of open ground through gardens, destroying fences and outhouses, and finally crashing into 30 Westland Road. Demolishing the house the aircraft exploded in flames, killing the pilot and Mrs Edith Brown who died instantly in the ruins of her home. The next door house, number 28, was also in flames and trapped in the doorway between the kitchen and the living room by the collapsed rear wall was Mrs Edith Hockey surrounded by fire.

Amongst the first to arrive at the scene of devastation was Reg Holland from his shop on the corner of Orchard Street, and George Hulbert, with his son Ron, from their Beer Street motor workshop. Together with Messrs Warton, Govier, Williams and Moulding, they fought to free Edith Hockey from the blazing wreckage but were forced back time after time by the smoke and flames. The Westland works firemen were quickly on the spot and soon after, the town's appliances arrived, followed by foam tenders from the Royal Naval Air Station at Yeovilton. Divisional Officer Charles Mitchell, commander of the Yeovil Fire Service, led the attempts to free Edith

Hockey and, as his men fought to keep the fire back, Station Officer Richards burrowed through the rubble to release her legs while Sub Officer Newman and Fireman Hardy worked from the opposite side of the débris. Station Officer Richards later recalled how he had came across a fluffy bundle, which for a moment he thought was a child but found was Mrs Hockey's little dog, who scampered away when he freed it. Dr J. C. McMaster, who had been at Westland that morning, hurried to the scene and, despite the horrific conditions, managed to administer a pain-killing morphia injection to the badly-burned Edith Hockey who was finally freed after half an hour's suffering. She was rushed to Yeovil hospital but sadly died two days later. The efforts of the fire crews saved the remaining two houses in the terrace and after two hours the flames were out.

Recalling the events of the morning, Mrs Arnold of 24 Westland Road told how she was preparing dinner for her brother and sister when the roar of the crash sent her diving for cover under her sewing machine. Recovering from the shock, she ran outside to find the area ablaze and made a futile attempt to fight the fire with buckets of water. 'It was a hopeless task,' she said. Another housewife, Mrs Hann at 32 Westland Road, told how she was preparing dinner when she heard a plane go over but took little notice as low-flying aircraft were commonplace. Shortly after there was a violent explosion as the Wyvern ploughed into the house next door.

Part of one of the aircraft's wings, complete with fuel tank, cartwheeled over the houses and struck the home of the Mills family at 16 Westland Road. Although the wall of the house was damaged, the fuel tank did not explode, and the only occupant at the time, the Mills baby, escaped unhurt, its mother having just popped out to see a neighbour.

At the inquest which followed, Westland's chief test pilot, Mr Harold Penrose, described the final moments of the doomed Wyvern. He said that the flight was a routine experimental test, and when he first saw the aircraft it was flying at about three hundred feet with both propellers stopped and the undercarriage retracted. It was apparent that Sq. Ldr Graves was in great difficulty in attempting to make a forced landing on the airfield before reaching the eastern perimeter. The Wyvern was travelling at well over two hundred miles an hour, but when the pilot realised he would overshoot he made a deeper dive which must have further increased his speed. It was a gamble whether he could get down and despite everything he tried, Mr Penrose believed that the Squadron Leader did not have a chance at the speed he was travelling.

A senior officer of the accident investigation branch of the Ministry of Civil Aviation stated that the Wyvern's engine had stopped when it crashed but despite a thorough examination of all the components it was not possible to discover whether this had been due to fuel starvation or some other cause.

Addressing the jury, the Deputy Coroner stated that he believed that once the pilot had realised he was in difficulties he had taken the only action he could to prevent the machine from dropping in the middle of the town with more disastrous consequences and that he must have known that he never had a chance. He thought it was a credit to test pilots that they felt it not only their duty but their honour to try and get the aircraft down so that any cause of difficulty could be discovered.

Verdicts of misadventure were returned on the four victims and the foreman of the jury stated that 'the pilot of the aircraft did everything humanly possible to bring the aircraft down on the airfield. We consider that he had so short a time in which to do anything that he did the best he could under the circumstances and that he realised that he was going to his death.'

In all 127 Westland Wyverns were built and the aircraft finally entered squadron service with the Fleet Air Arm in 1953. Wyverns flew in the Suez campaign in 1956, the only occasion when a British turbo-prop powered aircraft saw combat. It was the last conventional aircraft designed and built by Westland Aircraft.

TAUNTON'S MAD
MUNICIPAL MOMENTS

At the quarterly meeting of Taunton Borough Council held on the evening of Tuesday, 11 August 1896, Alderman Spiller presented the report of the committee responsible for the town's drainage and sanitation and remarked that at the previous week's committee meeting, Councillor Standfast had called the members 'a lot of fools and idiots'. The councillor had also accused the committee of proposing to buy land from their friends and were going to get a 'big haul' out of the deal. Alderman Spiller stated that he had been shocked and upset at the language, and the allegations were without a shadow of foundation.

Councillor Webber agreed with the alderman and went on to recall Councillor Standfast's actual words which were, 'What do we find! They said there was land to be had in every position, and then they bought land to benefit their friends and rob the poor. The committee must be fools and idiots to do it!' Because of this disgusting language Councillor Webber wished to be relieved from serving on any committee with Councillor Standfast.

Councillor Standfast, living up to his name, retorted that it was very fine for Councillor Webber to say that he had called the committee fools and idiots, but that very same councillor had threatened to screw his nose out of his face. To cries of 'order' he went on to shout that these were the words of Councillor Webber and he defied anyone to deny it! Councillor Webber responded by threatening to horse-whip his accuser who retorted that he was the one who had called the committee fools and idiots!

The town clerk, sensing that the meeting was about to degenerate into a shouting match, if not worse, said quite bluntly that Councillor Standfast had called the committee fools, idiots and rascals. The intervention from the respected chief official had the effect of silencing the outbursts, and apart from some muttering, normal business resumed.

They were at it again in 1903, when the Borough Council's meeting on 9 February closed with a shouting match between the mayor and Alderman Potter, the chairman of the Electric Lighting Committee. During the discussion of the Finance Committee's report, the mayor had contended that the general district rate should be paid on the electric light works and the water works, both of which belonged to the Borough Council. If this were done these undertakings would show much less profit than they did at present. Alderman Potter pointed out that if this suggestion was adopted it would be merely taking the money out of one pocket and putting it into another. The mayor exclaimed, in what was described as 'a loud tone,' that he was sorry to have to say that Alderman Potter was a man who was guilty of misrepresentation and deception in public matters. Alderman Potter indignantly denied this accusation but the mayor repeated it more vehemently and the alderman shouted that the mayor was a liar. Tempers were rising rapidly and in reply the mayor exclaimed, 'A more untruthful man I never met!'

The shouting match continued for a few more minutes and as the mayor left the room he called back to Alderman Potter, 'You're telling lies,' to which the latter replied, 'I'm not given to telling lies.' As a final shot the mayor shouted, 'You cannot help it,' and thus the meeting ended.

Were the electors of Taunton surprised and alarmed at the antics of their civic leaders? The answer must remain lost in the mists of time.

THE DAY THE
BALLOON DIDN'T GO UP

One of the highlights in Somerset over ninety years ago was the annual Amalgamated Friendly Societies fête which in August 1901 was held in the Home Field at Newton Farm, Yeovil. Most of the businesses in the town closed for the day and over 9000 people came by special trains, in carts, on bicycles and on foot from across Somerset and from the neighbouring towns and villages of Dorset.

The day broke dully, with a hint of rain in the air, but who cared, there would be parades, games, sports, performers, food and drink, and the thrilling main event would be the ascent of Professor Fleet in the largest hot air balloon in the world. The ascent was scheduled for three o'clock but by then the gentle breeze of the morning had turned into a strong gusty wind, and the departure was postponed until the evening. There were cries of disappointment from the expectant crowd but there was so much to see and do that Professor Fleet was quickly forgotten as the Three Smalleys gave exciting performances on the triple bars. There were gasps at the daring feats of Onda and Artel and their partners, Unda and Ovah, on the trapeze, while La Belle Emma thrilled the crowd with her wire-walking performances.

At tea time activity began again around the balloon, and the huge underground furnace was lit to provide the hot air. The filling operations began and slowly the balloon was inflated to its full height of 150 feet and was held down by forty men. In spite of a little swaying, all seemed to be going well and Professor Fleet took his seat in the sling from which he would parachute at the appropriate time. The ropes used for steadying the balloon were cut, but just before the signal was given to let go, there was a sudden gust of wind and the balloon heeled over. There was the sound of tearing fabric and the balloon collapsed, ripped from top to bottom.

To groans of disappointment, Professor Fleet supervised the recovery of the wreck and the fête committee went into emergency session to decide what to do next. Professor Fleet had brought two spare balloons and it was resolved that he should be asked to try again but this the intrepid aviator refused to do unless the committee undertook to pay for the damage done in his first attempt. The committe declined to give such an undertaking and the balloon spectacular was cancelled much to the frustration of the crowd, one of whom had to be ejected from the ground as he became more and more aggressive. Soon, however, the other entertainments took over and the day ended with a grand firework display provided by Messrs Brock.

Professor Fleet gave an interview to a reporter on one of the local papers and announced that the cost of the damage would be over £50. He said that the balloon was made from specially prepared light but strong material, known as balloon fabric, and was practically brand new. The Professor regretted that he had not been able to perform his stunts but he was not altogether surprised at what had happened. He stated that because of the high wind, he had not been happy to attempt the ascent but had only done so under pressure from the fête committee. The balloon had collapsed because just at the point when it was completely full of hot air, the wind had got underneath it, compressing the air and bursting the fabric. Professor Fleet said that in his ten years as a balloonist and parachutist, such a thing had never happened before.

There is a sequel to the story. In the autumn of 1901 Professor Fleet sued Messrs Atkins and Elliott, the joint secretaries of the fête committee, for £26 2s 0d which they had declined to pay because the contracted ascent did not take place. In their defence, Messrs Atkins and Elliott suggested that the balloon was defective, the weather not unfavourable, and that the Professor had no intention of making the ascent. Professor Fleet won his claim.

OF MURDERERS
AND HIGHWAYMEN

1 830 was a turbulent year in England, and South Somerset was no exception. The scent of political and parliamentary reform was in the air and the Duke of Wellington voiced the fears of many when he said, 'Beginning reform is beginning revolution.' There was widespread discontent in the countryside and 'Captain Swing' and his men were burning hayricks and smashing the machines which were seen, by many agricultural labourers, to threaten their already meagre livelihoods. Poverty was grinding and widespread and it was reported in February 1830 that 'at Castle Cary the population is under 1900 and there are 1000 names on the poor book receiving more or less of Parish pay.'

1830 was a violent year in South Somerset. James Lane, a small farmer living at the aptly named 'Deadman's Post' in the parish of Buckland St Mary, was found guilty and transported for life for the manslaughter of his twelve-year-old son John. The death of the boy followed years of abuse and brutality from his father. At Chard, John Russell killed Joan Turner and although he was sentenced to hang, the punishment was commuted to transportation to Australia for the rest of his natural life.

Mr Simeon Stuckey, a substantial builder of Chard, disappeared on his way home from supervising the new house being built for Mr Benjamin Hebditch in Stratton but despite a widespread search, his battered body lay undiscovered for several weeks in a wheat field in Dinngton. There is a slight air of mystery surrounding the builder's violent end – he was not robbed of the money he was known to be carrying and none of his personal effects, including a fob-watch, were taken. He was said to have had no enemies and was a leading member of the Chard Independent Church, so why was he ambushed and beaten to death? The murderer or murderers remain unknown to this day.

Travelling along the narrow roads and lanes after dark in South Somerset could be perilous as Mr Gilpin, a Crewkerne surgeon, discovered on a February evening on his way home from a visit to Martock. As the surgeon reached the Two Mile Stone approaching Crewkerne he saw from the corner of his eye a shadowy figure detach itself from the darkness of the bushes and suddenly there was a flash followed by a loud bang as a gun was fired straight at him. Mr Gilpin's head jerked as his hat was blown away by the shot and then his horse bolted at full speed down the road to Crewkerne. No more shots followed the fleeing rider and a few minutes later Mr Gilpin caught up with a cart being driven by Mr Mills, a local baker, who was accompanied by a friend. The two men needed no persuasion to return with the surgeon to hunt down the would-be assassin but by the time they arrived at the scene the man had disappeared into the night. Mr Gilpin's hat was recovered and showed what a lucky escape he had experienced. The ball had entered the hat just above the right side of his head and taking a slanting course had exited on the left side just under the crown; an inch lower and the surgeon would have been a dead man! On his arrival at Crewkerne, baker Mills told the authorities that as he passed the Two Mile Stone he had made out in the gloom the tall figure of a man wearing light-coloured clothes who appeared to be trying to hide something under his arm. A reward of £100 was offered for the apprehension and conviction of the attacker but he was never found.

The following month a Lieutenant Brown was robbed and severely injured near Stoke St Mary as he returned to Taunton. It was believed, however, that the Lieutenant was mistaken for his brother who was also travelling the same road carrying a large sum of money. Towards the end of 1830 there was an outbreak of highway robbery around Chard which culminated in an attack on John Clinch as he was returning from Taunton on the evening of 15 December. The victim was dragged from his horse, beaten and then robbed by three men. However John Clinch recognised one of his assailants and all three were quickly taken into custody. At the Assizes the highway robbers were convicted and transported to Australia for life.

THE THRASHING OF PROFESSOR WHITWORTH

The hall of the Literary Institution in Church Street, Yeovil, was full on the evening of Friday, 19 October, 1860 and the audience eagerly awaited the appearance of 'Professor' Whitworth and his entertaining lecture on Electro Biology. Professor Whitworth's previous lectures in Yeovil had been thoroughly enjoyed and everyone was certain that this evening would be no exception.

To applause, the Professor took the stage and called upon some young men from the audience to join him and assist with his experiments of Electro Biology. The volunteers were instructed to sit on the chairs provided and the proceedings began.

James Vincent was the first subject and after being asked by the Professor to stare at his hands the young man appeared to go slowly into a trance. After sniffing some chemicals placed in a handkerchief the Professor instructed James to go to a Mr Warry who was sitting in the front row, under the belief that he was a young lady, and kiss him. Without hesitation James ran over to Mr Warry and embraced him in an overwhelming show of affection. The audience cheered as the two fell and rolled on the floor but no offence was taken by the victim who joined in the performance with enthusiasm.

The next subject was a young man called Seward, a pupil teacher at Huish National School, and he was accordingly prepared by the Professor. As soon as he was entranced a member of the audience came forward with a piece of yellow soap and, presenting it to the young teacher, told him that it was a tasty piece of cheese. However, before he could begin to eat the soap, it was taken from him by Professor Whitworth.

How the events that followed began will always remain a mystery but what is certain is that young Seward appeared to be attracted by a Mr Donne, who was also sitting in the front row, and, advancing towards this gentleman, grasped him in an amorous manner. The alarmed Mr Donne resisted and as the Professor hurried over he shouted, 'Take him off, if you do not I will give you a thrashing!' As Professor Whitworth was leading his subject back to his seat, the enraged Mr Donne leapt up and laid about the lecturer with his walking stick landing three or four hard blows on his back. The hall erupted as the audience cheered and jeered at the spectacle of the irate Mr Donne belabouring the surprised Professor and, needless to say, at this moment the lecture came to an abrupt end.

Following a complaint to the police by the smarting Professor Whitworth, a charge of assault was laid against Mr Donne and the case came before the Borough magistrates on 6 November 1860.

The events of Friday, 19 October were recounted but despite a stout defence by the redoutable Mr Donne he was found guilty and fined £2 plus costs. The magistrates also turned their attention to young Seward, who had stated that he could remember nothing of the incident, and commented that as a pupil teacher he should not allow himself to be made a fool of in public.

The case caused much excitement in the town and a report appeared in a local newspaper that, in the course of a Professor's performance of Electro Biology in the county, a curious incident had occurred. It was reported that a boy had been mesmerised, restored to his senses and had then gone home where he had eaten his supper and retired to bed as usual. In the middle of the night his parents were woken by a noise coming from the kitchen and on going down to investigate found their son gnawing the bars of the grate. The Professor had to be called to restore the boy to 'his customary sane state of mind'. This, expounded the commentator, was 'an instance of the injurious effects of Electro Biology practically applied.'

THE STRANGE CASE OF THE POISONED BABY OF BATH

On the morning of Saturday, 7 June 1851 a genteelly-dressed, respectable-looking lady walked into James Searle's chemist shop at 28 Claverton Street, Bath, and enquired about the furnished apartments he had advertised to let. After inspecting the sitting-room and bedroom the lady, who had announced herself as Mrs Slater, agreed to take the rooms for a week and said that if her husband approved they would rent them for a month or maybe longer. Mrs Slater left only to return a few hours later with some luggage and took up residence.

Mrs Searle, the chemist's wife, commented to her husband that their new tenant was in an advanced stage of pregnancy but was obviously respectable, and they awaited the arrival of Mr Slater.

On the following Monday, Mr Slater, a well-dressed middle-aged gentleman arrived, and agreed to take the rooms for a month. Following a suggestion by the chemist's wife, Mr John Lawrence, a surgeon who lived three houses away, was engaged for Mrs Slater's imminent confinement, and during the morning of 10 June she gave birth to a healthy baby girl who was named Elizabeth. A nurse was engaged to assist Mrs Slater with baby Elizabeth and Mrs Searle's sister, Miss Elizabeth Grant, who was spending the summer in Bath, helped with the general chores.

At the end of June, Mr Slater announced that he would be taking his wife to London for an indefinite period, and would be quitting the rooms. However, as they could not take baby Elizabeth with them, it was agreed that the child should be looked after by Mrs Searle and the sum of £1 per week paid for its care.

On 4 July the Slaters left and when they returned a fortnight later they expressed their complete satisfaction with the care the baby was receiving and said how well she looked. Mr and Mrs Slater visited again on the 1 August and on being shown into the sitting room, they remained alone with the baby for the afternoon. At about six o'clock, the couple left but later that evening the infant became restless and then very sick and suffered violent diarrhoea. The following morning Mr Searle gave the baby a saline mixture after which it seemed much better and gradually recovered over the next few days.

About a week later Mrs Slater called again and as she handed the baby to its mother, Mrs Searle told her of the infant's illness. Mrs

Slater spent several hours alone with her daughter but following her departure the sickness and diarrhoea recurred. The chemist and his wife now began to harbour some suspicion that all was not well, but they found it difficult to believe that such a respectable and affectionate couple as the Slaters would do anything to harm the child. However they voiced their concern to Mr Evan Evans, a surgeon of their acquaintance who suggested that the baby should be sent to the country for a change of air. Miss Grant therefore took the child to stay with a cousin at Hilperton near Trowbridge.

On her next visit, Mrs Slater expressed some surprise that her baby was staying elsewhere, but made no further comment when told that this had been on medical advice. A few days later, the chemist received a letter from Mrs Slater stating that she required the baby to be brought back on Friday, 12 September as she would be coming to Bath on the Saturday.

On its return, the child seemed a little better and an attack of diarrhoea the day before was put down to changes in its food. Mr Lawrence, the surgeon, was called and found the baby looking thin, suffering from white mouth, with ulcers where its two eye-teeth would come through, and diarrhoea. The surgeon prescribed borax and honey for the white mouth and some powders for the diarrhoea.

On the Saturday Mrs Slater called as promised and spent some time nursing her child. She visited again on the following Monday, this time in company with her husband, who discussed the health of his baby daughter with Mr Searle and thought that she looked quite well. The chemist suggested that Mr Lawrence should continue to attend the child in view of its recent illness, but Mr Slater thought this to be unnecessary as he believed Mr Searle to be quite capable of treating his daughter.

The baby's health began to improve and on Saturday morning, 20 September, Mrs Slater came alone to Bath. She arrived just after eleven o'clock and spent some time nursing the child in the parlour. Mr Lawrence called and told Mrs Slater how ill her baby had been, but that he believed she was on the way to a full recovery providing the child was well cared for. During the rest of the day, Mrs Slater nursed Elizabeth and Mrs Searle carried on with her household duties. However, on one occasion, when going into the parlour, the chemist's wife noticed the baby putting its tongue in and out and pulling a face as if it was tasting something unpleasant but when she mentioned this, Mrs Slater said that the child had been a little sick and then wiped its mouth with her handkerchief. Mrs Slater remained until the late afternoon but a short while after she left the sickness and diarrhoea began again.

The Searles were becoming increasingly afraid that something was being given to the child but still could not bring themselves to accuse the genteel Mrs Slater of poisoning her own baby. On 1 October, Mr Searle wrote to Mrs Slater, c/o Mr Crosby, Solicitor, Bristol, telling her how ill the baby had been after her last visit but how she was improving following treatment from Mr Lawrence. He went on to say that if anyone other than his family had been nursing the child he would have thought that it was being treated badly or had something improper administered to it.

Three days later Mrs Slater was back again but the parlour was in use and as she wished to be alone with her child, she was shown to one of the bedrooms where they remained for most of the afternoon. Before she left, Mrs Slater told Mrs Searle that she would be visiting on the coming Monday with her husband and asked for the use of the parlour or a bedroom. The sickness and diarrhoea began again that evening and as the baby seemed to be in great pain, Mr Lawrence was called and did his best to treat the frightening symptoms. Mrs Searle also gave the surgeon the two teats which had been prepared by her husband and used on the feeding bottle over the past few weeks.

Events now moved quickly. The Searles' diffidence had vanished for they were certain that the baby was being poisoned by its mother and they went to the police. Inspector John Norris of the Bath Police, and Eliza Lyons, a female searcher, kept out of sight when Mrs Slater arrived at 28 Claverton Street on 7 October, a day later than indicated, and without her husband. The inspector instructed Mrs Searle not to leave the mother alone with the baby while he watched through the blinds of the window in the wall separating the shop from the parlour. However, the chemist's wife was called from the parlour and during the short time she was absent, Mrs Slater went out of the policeman's view. On Mrs Searle's return, the two women and the baby went upstairs to one of the bedrooms followed by the inspector and his female searcher. Entering the bedroom the inspector informed Mrs Slater that he was here to take her into custody on suspicion of having administered something to her child. Despite her pleadings that they should wait until her husband arrived on the three o'clock train from Bristol, Mrs Slater was placed in a cab and conveyed to the police station. Here she was searched and although nothing incriminating was found on her person, her gloves and pocket were taken for more detailed examination.

Shortly after Mrs Slater was taken into custody, the child was violently sick and despite the efforts of Mr Lawrence its condition deteriorated and baby Elizabeth died on 11 October; the case of suspected poisoning became one of murder.

Now a scandal broke. 'Mrs Slater' was none other than Miss Elizabeth Catherine Lewis, of 5 Exeter Buildings, Redland, a former governess and member of a very respectable Bristol family while 'Mr Slater' was Mr Thomas Crosby, a prosperous solicitor, of St John's Bridge, Bristol. Under their true identities the pair were brought before the Bath magistrates,who, after a lengthy investigation, were satisfied that the baby had been systematically poisoned by the administration of arsenic and sent the couple for trial at the next Somerset Assizes.

The local newspapers quickly provided their readers with some tasty morsels about Miss Elizabeth Catherine Lewis. The *Bath Herald* disclosed, somewhat enigmatically, that:

From the contents of the letters found in possession of the prisoner, it appears she that she has been quite a traveller in her day, and among other places she has visited are the West India islands, calling at Barbadoes, Jamaica, etc. The letters – or more properly speaking some of these – contained a few rather amusing and amorous statements, but nothing, we believe could tend to prove that the prisoner has been guilty of the crime of which she stands charged. These letters came from various parts of the world; and it must be confessed that one of them shows that some gentlemen in Bristol are not the 'Joseph' they wish their better halves so believe; but no doubt they will place such 'little affairs' under the head of 'gallantry'.

The *Bristol Mirror* revealed that:

at the close of the proceedings before the magistrates on Thursday, the prisoner was taken to a private room in the Guildhall, where she had an interview with a female who had charge of another child of hers ... We understand that the other child of the prisoner above alluded to, is the illegitimate offspring of a gentleman of some property in the West Indies. The prisoner had resided for several years in Barbadoes, where she went out in the capacity of a governess, her accomplishments peculiarly fitting her for a situation of the kind.

The trial of Thomas Crosby and Elizabeth Catherine Lewis opened at the Assizes in Taunton before Mr Justice Erle on Monday,

5 April 1852, with Mr Hodges and Mr Saunders prosecuting, Mr Stone and Mr Cole defending for Mr Crosby and Mr Sergeant Kinglake and Mr Phinn for Miss Lewis.

Both prisoners pleaded not guilty. Opening for the prosecution, Mr Hodges told the court that the prisoners were charged with the wilful murder of a child, the daughter of the female prisoner, whom he believed was an unmarried person. He then outlined the events which had led up to the death of the child and which, in the opinion of the medical witnesses and confirmed by post-mortem examination, had been caused by the administration of poison. Mr Hodges stated that he would not endeavour to draw any ingenious conclusions or make ingenious suggestions in relation to the facts of the case but he would leave it to the jury to make their decision from the evidence he would lay before them.

The first witness was the chemist's wife, Mrs Mary Searle, who recalled the birth and short life of baby Elizabeth Slater and how her suspicions had grown during the months the child had been in her care. The incidents of violent sickness and diarrhoea following the visits of Miss Lewis and Mr Crosby were recounted in detail and these were crucial to the prosecution.

However, all the evidence was circumstantial, no one had seen the administration of arsenic and none had been found in the possession of either prisoner. A guilty verdict would mean execution for both prisoners and therefore the jury would have to be convinced beyond all reasonable doubt that they had committed the awful crime.

The defence set out to discredit the evidence of the prosecution's witnesses and to sow seeds of doubt. Under cross-examination by Mr Sergeant Kinglake, Mrs Searle agreed that Miss Lewis had been a fond and attentive mother and that both women had been on good terms. The baby had not been fed at the breast but dry nursed and the witness and her sister, Miss Grant, had prepared its food at all times. Mrs Searle agreed that there had been problems in feeding the child who rejected milk without water, gruel and the arrowroot which she obtained from her husband's shop. She had tried other foods, some of which the baby had taken reluctantly and some of which had been rejected. The witness confirmed that she helped her husband in the shop and dispensed medicines but in no way could she have contaminated the baby's food. Mrs Searle agreed that the teats used on the feeding bottle were prepared in the shop and so were the medicines prescribed by Mr Lawrence. She was closely cross-examined about past instances when Mr Searle had supposedly made errors in some prescriptions but could not recollect that her

BURIALS in the Parish of *Stogursey*
in the County of *Somerset* in the Year 18*17*

Name.	Abode.	When buried.	Age.	By whom the Ceremony was performed.
William Brewing No. 89.	Stogursey,	1817 9th October	*Infant*	Wm Dawes Curate
Edward Thomas No. 90.	Culverstreet	11th October	61.	Wm Dawes Curate
A Man unknown found drowned on No. 91.	the Beach at Stolford on Tuesday the 25th November	27th November	—	John Dawes Curate
A Woman unknown found drowned on No. 92.	the Beach at Stolford on Wednesday the 26th Novbr.	27th November	—	John Dawes Curate
Solomon Norton No. 93.	Stolford,	1818. 6th January	78.	John Dawes Curate
Ann Brown No. 94.	Stogursey,	6th January	62.	John Dawes Curate
James Hawtree No. 95.	Stogursey,	14th January	50	John Dawes Curate
Mary Andrews No. 96.	Stogursey	14th March	76	John Dawes Curate

THE LOSS OF THE WILLIAM AND MARY

The Register of the Parish of Stogursey records the burial, on 27 November 1817, of the bodies of an unknown man and woman, believed to have been victims from the wreck of the William and Mary.

THE BRUTES OF BRIDGWATER

In January 1823, a poor apprentice chimney sweep dies and his master and mistress are charged with murder. An early nineteenth century lithograph of the Cornhill, Bridgwater.

A LIFE LOST FOR A KISS
*Near this spot, late in the evening of 13 August 1857, the driver fell
from the tender of the 'Leopold' railway engine and received fatal
injuries – the question was 'Why'?*

WESTON PIER DESTROYED BY FIRE
*Weston-super-Mare's Grand Pier Pavilion, pictured here shortly after
its completion, was totally destroyed in a fire on 13 January 1930.*

THE SHOOTING AT THE ROCK HOUSE INN
James Pearce's visit to the Rock House Inn, near Curry Mallet, on a May morning in 1814 would end in a nightmare. The former inn is now a private residence.

THE SOUTH SOMERSET BREAD RIOTS
On 14 November 1867, over three hundred rioters stormed through South Petherton, shown here in a rare nineteenth century photograph, violently protesting at the high price of bread.

A PROPHECY OF DISASTER

On Good Friday morning, 1879, an intrepid local journalist took the rough road up to Ham Hill to report first hand on the prophesied disaster. (Author).

THE SHOOTING OF LORD GLASTONBURY'S GAMEKEEPER

The peaceful scene of Compton Dundon in the early nineteenth century would be shattered by the shooting of a gamekeeper.

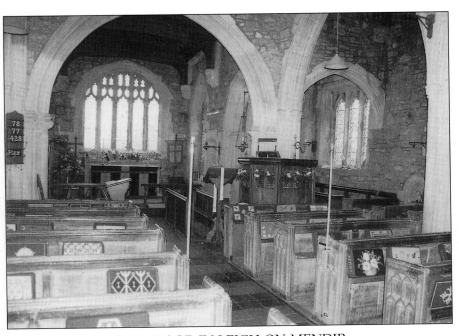

BAD BLOOD IN LEIGH-ON-MENDIP

'...there was a tremendous crash and the congregation stared in horror as the Reverend Mahon slumped semi-conscious in his pulpit, covered in blood and smoke drifted up to the roof above the north aisle of St Giles Church...'

A SHORT STEP AND A LONG DROP

'... after retorting "I know Yeovil better than you do!" Mr Edginton stepped out into the gathering darkness onto the parapet of the bridge and dropped 25 feet into the stream below.' (The safety railings are a later addition).

THE ERRAND BOY'S COURAGE
*The drinking trough bought by the people of Chard in memory
of the selfless courage of Lawrence Hussey.*

THE FALL OF A WYVERN
*The scene of devastation following the crash of the Wyvern turboprop fighter
into houses in Westland Road, Yeovil on 31 October 1949.*

THE DAY THE BALLOON DIDN'T GO UP
Unlike the balloon, shown about to be launched at the Amalgamated Friendly Societies' Fête in 1899, the ascent at the 1901 Fête was doomed to failure.

THE STRANGE CASE OF THE POISONED BABY OF BATH
Claverton Street, Bath, on a wet day one hundred-and-forty-eight years after the tragic events of 1851.

In Loving Memory

OF

AMOS CANN,

WHO DIED MARCH 1891 AGED 24 YEARS.

IN LIFE BELOVED IN DEATH LAMENTED

You that are young behold and see
How quickly death has conquered me;
Its fatal stroke it was too strong,
It cut me off while I was young;
The God above He knows for why
That in my youth I was to die.

THE BLIZZARD OF 1891
*The headstone in Exford churchyard in memory of Amos Cann
who was caught out in the great blizzard and froze to death.*

A DASTARDLY OUTRAGE

'One of the plate glass windows of Messrs Price & Son's showroom was damaged, apparently by a bullet....' In this contemporary photograph of Princes Street, Yeovil, the showroom is the second property from the right edge of the picture.

AN OCTOBER STORM
A contemporary print of workers repairing the damage at Minehead caused by the fierce storm of October 1859.

RICHARD HEWLETT –
UNSUCCESSFUL HIGHWAYMAN
Although described by the Taunton Courier *as 'the ferocious highwayman' Richard Hewlett was captured by his badly injured victim.*

THE FATAL FIRING

The tragic events of 2 August 1866 during the firing of the celebration cannon were enacted on the left bank of the River Parrett looking towards Langport's Great Bow Bridge.

EIGHT ESCAPE FROM PLYMOUTH

The town of Chard at the time of the capture of the deserter John Higgins.

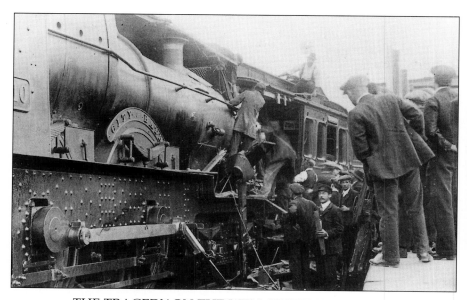

THE TRAGEDY ON THE WEYMOUTH EXCURSION

'The 'City of Bath' ploughed like a remorseless piston into the last carriage ...'
Rescuers work frantically to free victims from the wreckage of the last
carriage of the Weymouth excursion.

SOMETHING IN THE ATTIC

The news of the gruesome find in the attic of 'The Green' quickly spread through
Somerton, shown here in a photograph taken at the turn of the century.

MR MORFORD AND THE GERMAN SPY

'The German Spy' was 'arrested' in Shepton Mallet at the Hare and Hounds Hotel, shown on the right of the picture.

THE PASSING OF TREVOR HOYLE
'One of the air raid wardens on duty in Westland Road saw Trevor turn down the cul-de-sac where he lived – about ten minutes later the bombs fell.' Fifty years later in 1991, the houses have been rebuilt and peace has long since returned.

STAND AND DELIVER!
The Ship Inn, West Stour, where in 1871 the young highwaymen, Charlie Cross and Tommy Hinks, were arrested by Constable Devenish.

FIVE WEIRD STORIES – BURIED ALIVE?

Was Richard Parsons buried alive in Merriott churchyard in 1870?

YEOVIL CEMETERY HOLDS A SECRET
*A Luftwaffe aerial reconnaissance photograph of Yeovil taken on
15 October 1940, the week following the air raids, shows the Westland
Aircraft Works at the top right of the photograph to be undamaged.*
(Photograph supplied by Nigel J. Clarke Publications).

husband had been recommended by a colleague to throw away some drugs which had become dangerously mixed. The witness also denied knowledge of where the chemist kept his supply of arsenic.

Mrs Searle recalled giving the teat to Mr Lawrence following the illness of the baby on 20 September and giving him a second which she had initially thrown under the fire grate in the kitchen. Defence counsel continued to press the witness on the feeding methods, the preparation of the medicines for the child and alluded to the possibility of the food becoming accidently contaminated with small quantities of arsenic from the shop.

After three hours of intense questioning on the events of the months from June to October 1851, Mrs Searle left the witness box where she was followed by her sister, Elizabeth Grant. Her evidence added little save to confirm how the health of the child had deteriorated on its return from Hilperton on 12 September. She recalled, however, that on one occasion when she had gone into the bedroom she had found the baby's lips moving as if it had been eating something and the next day it had diarrhoea. The witness agreed that Miss Lewis had always appeared affectionate towards the child.

Mr James Searle, the chemist, now took the stand and stated that he had been in business at 28 Claverton Street for ten years and had dispensed medicines for over twenty-five years. He described the illness of the infant and detailed the medicines he had prepared. The chemist stated that he kept the arsenic in his shop in a stone jar clearly labelled 'arsenic-poison' but that it was hidden away and only he knew where. The top of the jar was tied down and the wooden spoon he used was kept inside; the jar was never kept with the other bottles. Mr Searle said that he employed two apprentices to assist in the shop and dispense medicines but neither would touch arsenic without his supervision or instruction. He could not recall the allegations of incorrect dispensing or that he had been keeping his drugs irregularly. Some eighteen months ago he had signed a declaration that he would not sell arsenic to anyone other than a medical man and in the previous September he had supplied a small quantity to Mr Lawrence, the surgeon.

Inspector John Norris of the Bath police gave details of the arrest of Miss Lewis. Under cross-examination the officer confirmed that he had found no arsenic in the parlour or bedroom at 28 Claverton Street and none had been discovered when Miss Lewis was searched at the police station. A thorough search of her home at Redland, where she lived with her mother and sister, had produced nothing incriminating.

Inspector Alexander Brown of the Bath police, testified that on 6

October he had gone to the house of Mr Searle and in his presence the nightgown and a foul napkin were removed from the child and, after wrapping the articles and sealing them in a brown paper parcel, he had delivered them two days later to Mr Herapath, the analytical chemist, at Bristol.

The female searcher, Eliza Lyons, stated that when Miss Lewis was arrested she had put on her gloves as she left for the police station. Nothing suspicious was found on the prisoner when she was searched and her gloves and pocket were sent to Mr Herapath for examination.

The surgeon, Mr Joseph Lawrence, now entered the witness box and stated that he had been in practice in Bath for about three-and-a-half years. He had attended Miss Lewis when she was confined and continued to be her medical practitioner during the time she lived with the Searles at 28 Claverton Street. Although her child was small, it was healthy, but when he saw the child on its return from the country on 12 September it was suffering from white mouth, there were ulcers on the upper jaw where the eye-teeth usually came through, there was an ulcer on the buttocks and also diarrhoea. The surgeon stated that he prescribed medicine for the white mouth and diarrhoea and attended the baby until the 18 September by which time it was much better. He saw the child again two days later on the occasion of Miss Lewis's visit and she had seemed very concerned about its health. Mr Lawrence had told her that the baby had been very ill but that with care it should make a full recovery. As he left, he saw Miss Lewis lean over the child and say 'My dear, I must get your father to settle down and we must have you home.' The baby was ill during the evening of 20 September and much worse on the 22nd, but began to improve and by 2 October the surgeon thought it to be quite well. However Mr Lawrence recalled being sent for on 6 October and when he found the child to be worse than he had ever seen it. The white mouth and the diarrhoea had returned and the expression on the infant's face indicated that it was suffering great pain. He prescribed for irritation of the bowels and when he saw the child again the next day before he left for Bristol it seemed a little better.

At Bath Station he happened to meet Miss Lewis coming from the train in a very distressed state exclaiming that she had come to Bath again because of a letter she had received from the Searles saying that the baby was very ill and that he had taken one of the teats from the feeding bottle for examination. The surgeon tried to calm Miss Lewis and explained that he wanted to examine the teat as there was something the matter with the baby's teeth; he also told her that the child seemed a little better. Mr Lawrence went on recount that on his return in the evening he had found to his surprise and alarm that the baby was very ill. He continued to attend the baby but despite his medical efforts, it died on 11 October.

Mr Lawrence stated that on 13 October he had carried out a post-mortem examination of the child in the presence of several medical colleagues and Mr Herapath. He explained in detail the results of the examination which showed the body to be greatly emaciated; there were rashes on the buttocks and an ulcer in the groin was dissected and given to Mr Herapath for examination. The appearance of the internal organs was consistent with arsenic being administered at intervals and in small quantities. The liver, stomach and intestinal canal were removed and delivered to Mr Herapath in sealed jars for examination. Mr Lawrence went on to say that Mr John Tyler, a Bath chemist, had tested the two teats given to him by Mrs Searle and a small quantity of crystal found in them had been given to Mr Herapath for analysis.

Cross-examined by Mr Sergeant Kinglake, the surgeon agreed that Miss Lewis had always appeared very attentive to her child and although he understood the infant had been left in his medical care, he had not been consulted before it was taken to Hilperton. Mr Lawrence admitted that during his medical practice he had never seen a case of death from arsenical poisoning and therefore could not speak from experience. Mr Sergeant Kinglake then asked how much arsenic would be needed to cause death and the surgeon considered that three or four grains would be fatal to a man and half an eighth or the sixteenth of a grain would be dangerous to a three- or four-month-old child. A quarter of a grain might be administered from time to time without being immediately fatal but he could not say whether a smaller amount would have a similar effect. Mr Lawrence agreed that diarrhoea could result from food being given to a child when its stomach was in a naturally irritated state. He stated that although the baby had required care in the food it was given it had not suffered from diarrhoea in the first month.

The surgeon, Mr Evan Evans, was called and stated that he had attended the baby at the request of Mr Searle and found it suffering the symptoms described by Mr Lawrence. On his advice the child had been taken into the country for the benefit of its health. Cross-examined the surgeon admitted that he had only seen the baby on one occasion but pointed out that he had considerable experience of diseases in children. He stated that white mouth need not be accompanied by irritability of the stomach and although he had seen several cases of arsenic overdose, he had not seen it in a child.

All eyes were now focused on Mr William Herapath, an analytical chemist with a formidable reputation. His evidence could put a rope around the necks of the prisoners. The chemist testified that on 7 October he had received from Mr Lawrence a sealed jar containing two napkins, and on the eighth, a parcel with a foul napkin and a child's bedgown was delivered by Inspector Brown. He found slight traces of arsenic in the marks of vomit on the bedgown, and on the foul napkin and the two napkins received from Mr Lawrence also showed traces of arsenic. Examination of the child's liver, stomach and intestines produced slight traces of arsenic and traces were found in the ulcer dissected from the groin; there was a slight trace in a patch of skin taken from the rash on the buttocks. Mr Herapath stated that he had found no arsenic in solid form and the quantity taken must therefore have been minute. A dose sufficient to destroy life would have produced a very different appearance in the organs. He could form no judgement of how long the arsenic had been administered but it must have been long enough to be absorbed into the system. However all the appearances were those of small quantities administered several times and, generally speaking, the rash on the child's buttocks could be the result of slow poison.

Mr Herapath then turned to the crystals received from Mr Lawrence which, on being dissolved, produced arsenic. If this had been administered through the teat a portion would adhere to it. Cross-examined by Mr Sergeant Kinglake, the chemist admitted that he had not obtained the twentieth part of a grain from all of the child's body and the quantity of arsenic must have been almost inappreciable. He agreed that he could detect the millionth part of a grain but his test of Miss Lewis's gloves and pocket had produced no signs of arsenic. The Bath chemist, Mr John Tyler, testified that he had produced a small quantity of arsenic from the two teats but agreed that the quantity was too minute to measure.

The case for the Crown was now complete and Mr Stone rose to address the jury on behalf of Mr Crosby. He stated that for thirty years his client had carried on an extensive business as a solicitor in Bristol, esteemed for his skill, his humanity and his integrity. Mr Stone then summarised the facts of the case against Mr Crosby and asked whether any jury could take away his life on such scant evidence? Mr Stone then called a procession of witnesses who all testified to Mr Crosby's integrity and excellent character.

Mr Sergeant Kinglake now addressed the jury and contended that his client Miss Elizabeth Lewis had no motive to commission the dreadful offence with which she stood charged. She had already one child living in her own neighbourhood, and therefore the feeling which sometimes made unfortunate mothers wish to kill their child did not exist with her. In this case, the child was comfortably placed, its father had showed every wish to protect it and had ample means to do so, the mother was fondly attached to it, and yet the jury were asked to believe that she had poisoned it by slow degrees. It was stated that the death of the infant had been caused by the administration of arsenic by the female prisoner, but this charge was only founded upon the inference that the child had been sick and had diarrhoea on several occasions after being visited by its mother. The answer to this could be summed up in very few words – first, the absence of a motive and, second, the prisoner's conduct. To the first he had already referred, and to the second, it was a strange coincidence that every witness confirmed that from the time the child was born to the moment of its death, the conduct of the mother was kind, gentle, tender and affectionate; bursting at times into tears at its sufferings, anxious for its relief, and sending for a medical man and urging him repeatedly to cure the child of its sufferings. Throughout all her visits – the object of which, according to the prosecution, was the gradual murder of the child – she had never concealed her actions. The child had been sent away while suffering the symptoms and during that time the prisoner had not seen it, yet the infant had returned home still suffering from diarrhoea. Mr Lawrence had seen it before the mother came, and had administered medicines. It was manifest that the child was sickly and was incapable of taking ordinary food, a variety of which had been tried without effect. Its stomach was irritable and rejected food and thus diarrhoea was caused. Then again, was it consistent with the idea of guilt, to suppose that, after the 'warnings' given in the communications of Mr Searle that the prisoner would have continued to give poison to the child? That was too strange an hypothesis. There was the insinuation that while she was in the corner of the parlour she gave the child poison. But she was searched minutely, the parlour was inspected, and no trace of arsenic was found. Where did it come from then? How could she have administered the smallest quantity of arsenic to the child in the space of half a minute, with eyes upon her, if no sign of it could be found? Mr Herapath said that he could discover the millionth part of a grain, and had the prisoner had any on her fingers, he would have been able to find it in the gloves she had worn. Nothing had been found. In conclusion Mr Sergeant Kinglake suggested that the greater probability was that the arsenic came from the shop and got upon the teats by which the child was fed.

Witnesses were now called on behalf of Miss Lewis and all said how kind and affectionate she was to children.

The judge, Mr Justice Erle, turned to the jury and began his summing up. He stated that the prisoners stood indicted of the wilful murder of the child of the female prisoner. Although they were both indicted, in effect the prisoner Thomas Crosby was charged as an accessory before the fact. The jury had been told by the prosecution that their duty was one of immense importance because a great crime had been committed and the public had the right to be protected. Also it was of the deepest importance to the prisoners that they should not be convicted unless the evidence was such that the jury were left in no reasonable doubt of their guilt. With regard to the charge of murder by poison, this required the most careful consideration because it was a crime which was usually committed in great secrecy. The present case required patient deliberation because it was assumed on the part of the prosecution that death had been caused, not by the administration of one dose, but at several times in minute doses, so as to gradually produce a fatal result. There were three questions for the jury to decide. First, were they satisfied that the death of the child had been caused by arsenical poisoning? If not, then this would be the end of the inquiry, but if they were satisfied, the second question would be whether it was administered by the prisoner Elizabeth Lewis, and if they considered that it had been, the third question was whether Thomas Crosby was an accessory. Mr Justice Erle then went through the evidence pointing out where it applied to the questions he had posed both for and against the prisoners.

The jury took only only a few minutes to return verdicts of not guilty. Elizabeth Lewis, who had remained heavily veiled throughout the trial, collapsed in a faint and was carried from the dock, followed by her lover, Thomas Crosby, who was reported to have 'felt acutely the very painful situation in which he stood and his mental agony was evident from the tears he profusely shed.'

And so the middle-aged solicitor and his mistress, the wayward governess, left the court and no doubt provided the genteel drawing rooms and salons of fashionable Bath and Bristol with some interesting gossip for some time to come.

THE BLIZZARD OF 1891

February, 1891 was an extraordinarily fine and dry month, but March lived up to its reputation of coming in like a lion when a blizzard swept in on a north-east wind on Monday, 9 March. The storm raged all day and on Monday evening its fury increased. There was a lull on Tuesday morning but then the wind picked up again and blew furiously until Wednesday. The south-western counties suffered the most and right across Somerset roads and railways were blocked by huge snow drifts, towns and villages were isolated and huge seas battered the coast.

Taunton was severely affected and on Tuesday evening a train carrying the Duke of Edinburgh to Plymouth was not allowed to leave the town and he was put up in the Railway Hotel until normal services resumed on Thursday morning.

There was drama in the Wells and Shepton Mallet areas as graphically described in the *Western Gazette* on 13 March:

Snow and wind raged together with the violence of a hurricane from Monday afternoon to Wednesday morning and the full effects were felt on Tuesday. The trains to Wells and the neighbouring towns of Glastonbury and Shepton Mallet arrived safely at their respective destinations on Monday night, and the 8.30 goods train from Wells to Chippenham was despatched at 9.30 accompanied by two engines – the relief engine to go so far as Witham and then return; this engine, however, did not leave Witham till one o'clock a.m., and after going a few miles and reaching Wanstrow, it became embedded in the snow and had not been released on Wednesday. The driver (Reeves) after assuring himself of the hopelessness of his position, sought shelter in the village of Wanstrow. Equally unpleasant was the experience of some travellers to Bristol on Tuesday morning, when the 7.20 train left Wells on time. Wookey and Lodge Hill were safely reached, but after proceeding a mile and a half from Lodge Hill the train became firmly embedded in the snow. It was then not more than eight o'clock in the morning, and as it was impossible to go forward an effort was made to return, but the distance back to Lodge Hill, short though it was, was not covered till quarter to five o'clock. One of the passengers to Bristol was Mr Salisbury from Keward, so that he and those in charge of the train were snowed up for over nine hours before they returned to the friendly shelter at Lodge Hill. Things too had not gone smoothly with Mr Salmon, the station master, for the wind had thrown the chimney of his dwelling house across the roof, and he with his wife and family had to seek the shelter of the station and convert the waiting room into a dining and sitting room by day and a bedroom by night. At about eleven o'clock on Tuesday, Mr Randall, the station master at Wells, instructed drivers Biggs and Richards to get their engines ready to proceed if possible to the rescue of Reeves. At one o'clock both engines had got up steam, and at ten minutes past one Mr Randall, with a number of men, made a start in the midst of a blinding hurricane of wind and snow. Several heavy storms were encountered on the way. Within a mile of Shepton Mallet, and practically within sight of the station, both engines came to a sudden stop, being tightly wedged in a huge drift of snow. A notice board on which the legend 'All goods trains must stop dead here' had a grim significance, for the engines were indeed stopped 'dead' and there seemed all probability of a long stop. The situation was anything but cheerful, the wind was howling and surging round the engines and driving the snow with terrific force. Time after time the valves of both engines were opened and full steam put on, but so firmly were the 'iron steeds' held that even with this force behind them they remained unmovable. Men were then set to dig the engines out, but it was not till nearly two hours detention that their efforts were successful. The time was spent on an elevated and bleak spot, the whole surroundings of the warring elements realistically suggestive of Siberian weather. When free, it was found impossible to reach Shepton Mallet station, which under ordinary circumstances was certainly not more that a three minutes run, so Mr Randall gave the order to return home, which was safely reached, after a cautious down hill journey, just before four o'clock. All efforts to open the Witham branch were then abandoned, and the line remained blocked the whole of Wednesday.

The letters from Wells are sent by mail cart to Shepton Mallet and thence by Somerset and Dorset Railway to Bath and the driver on Monday night had a rough time of it and only reached Shepton Mallet under extreme difficulty. Several times during his perilous drive he found himself in the hedge.

On Tuesday night the road was so blocked that he could not bring his cart, and he returned to Wells with only the horses. With such dreadful snowstorms usually follow loss of life, solitary instances perhaps here and there, but none the less sad. The report of one death has already come to hand. Between nine and ten o'clock on Wednesday morning, two men named James Lane and George Trivett found the body of a man near Hunters Lodge, Priddy. The body was completely buried in the snow, the head only being visible. The deceased is supposed to be Arthur White, aged about sixty, a farrier and a native of Glastonbury. He had been to Compton Martin on the Monday and was evidently returning home when overcome by the storm he sank exhausted to rest and to die.

Some houses at Castle Cary were buried in huge drifts and the occupants could only be released from their snowy prisons by neighbours digging them out; in one case the snow was so deep that the family could only be provisioned through an upstairs window.

Mr Elswood, the driver of a waggon and two horses belonging to Messrs Mitchell & Co., had a lucky escape when he became snowbound on the high road between Yarcombe and Chard. In desperation he spent the night between his horses and was kept from dying of exposure by the warmth of the two animals.

On Exmoor a young farmer was not so fortunate. Amos Cann set out from Porlock to walk home to Exford as the storm began and he disappeared. For some time the depth of snow on the moor prevented search parties from setting out to find him but on 26 March the young man's coat was discovered; it was supposed he had thrown it away so as to be more able to battle through the blizzard; his body was found the following day. He was buried in Exford churchyard where his headstone can be seen today just inside the main gate.

A DASTARDLY OUTRAGE

The general election of 27 January 1910 was hard fought and no more so than in the Liberal stronghold of the Yeovil Division where Sir Edward Strachey had been regularly returned to parliament since 1892. Sir Edward's Conservative opponent, the Hon. Aubrey Herbert, reduced the Liberal majority from almost 2000 at the 1906 election to 511 and in the 1911 bye-election, following Sir Edward's elevation to the peerage, the Conservatives did win the seat.

The poll in Yeovil on that January day in 1910 was the heaviest ever, and it was reported that by mid-day well over two-thirds of the electorate had voted – however the adult franchise was much smaller than today and most women were denied this fundamental right. The total turn out was ninety per cent with one Conservative travelling all the way from Rome to vote and a Liberal voter journeyed from Holland. On the eve of polling the Liberals processed through the town, behind a brass band which was said to have played only one tune because it knew no others. The crowd was followed by a legion of small boys, bearing the party red, and shouting as only small boys can. At the tail of this hullabaloo was a carriage, drawn by two horses, in which sat Lady Strachey accompanied by Mr C.W. Pittard. In opposition the Conservatives held a rally in the Prince's Street Assembly Rooms where the floor and stage were filled with enthusiastic supporters singing the Tariff Reform song and cheering speeches by local dignitaries.

During the evening following the declaration of the result the Conservatives, buoyed up by their good showing, held a demonstration in the Assembly Rooms in Princes Street where they were addressed by the Hon. Aubrey Herbert. Many partisan songs were sung and speeches made, after which everyone went noisily home through the streets.

What happened later that night was reported the next day by the *Western Gazette* under the headline 'A Dastardly Outrage'. The indignant townsfolk were told that late on Thursday night, following the Conservative demonstration in the Assembly Rooms, one of the plate glass windows of Messrs Price & Sons' showroom which adjoined the Constitutional Club in Princes Street, was damaged, apparently by a bullet. The hole on the outside of the glass was the size of a miniature rifle bullet and the piece punched from the inside was found 42 feet away at the back of the showroom indicating that the bullet had been fired from a high velocity weapon. The missile had grazed a showcard and ricocheted off a pillar but a detailed search failed to locate the bullet which had probably disintegrated.

The experts called in to investigate were of the opinion that the height of the hole and the direction of flight suggested that a bullet had been discharged from a passing vehicle, the noise of which would drown the sound of the shot, and which accounted for no one reporting the incident. Mr Priest, the shop manager, stated that he had heard nothing and noticed nothing when he closed down late that evening. The newspaper reported that 'a significant fact is that the window is next to the Conservative Club, and it is freely suggested that the shot was put through the shop window in mistake for that of the Club. If fired intentionally, and it is difficult to say how it could have been an accident, it was a dastardly thing to do, as the force behind the bullet was sufficient to have instantly killed anyone in its path.'

The culprit was never found.

PLAYING CARDS ON SUNDAY

The four boys huddled together on the banks of the Hendford Brook at Dodham in Yeovil were obviously up to no good on that October Sunday in 1890. Fearing that an illegal act was being committed Police Constable Horler secreted himself nearby and from his vantage point by the Dodham Bridge which crossed the Great Western Railway Company's track, south of the town station, he listened and observed. What he saw and heard during the next hour and a half was sufficient for the full vigour of the law to be invoked and PC Horler pounced.

William Berkeley, Edwin Pennell, Joseph Maniford, Charles Dodge and William Dodge, described 'as boys', appeared before the town magistrates charged with playing with cards and coins in a public place on Sunday, 12 October 1890. With the exception of Edwin Pennell, who said it was all lies and that he was not guilty, the boys pleaded guilty.

PC Horler told the court that on the Sunday in question he had concealed himself near Dodham Bridge and heard the defendants say, 'I'm one, I'm two, I'm three,' and so on. He saw Charles Dodge take up the money and put it in his pocket. Pennell who was dealing the cards, took up the next lot of money, while the next pile was taken by William Dodge. At this time Joseph Maniford came up and when invited to join in the game had said, 'Aye.' At this Pennell interrupted stating that this was a lie because Maniford could not speak which caused some laughter in the court.

PC Horler continued and stated that he had rushed in among the defendants and picked up the cards before they could hide them. With exception of Pennell the boys had fled in panic and Charles Dodge had jumped into the river! The constable stated that he could see and hear quite clearly what was going on as he was hiding only about nineteen feet away. In his defence Edwin Pennell called a Miss Rake who said that she had seen him lying on the grass and a boy named Alfred Norris leaning on him so that he could not have been playing cards. She went on to say that Joseph Maniford was not there for more than a minute. It had been between three and four o'clock when she had seen the defendants. PC Horler, recalled, stated that he had watched the boys for an hour-and-a-half from half past one to three o'clock. Miss Rake went on to say that she had seen the policeman take up the money and the cards and saw Edwin Pennell turn out his pockets to show that he had no cards in his possession.

Alfred Norris now testified that he had joined the boys at about three o'clock and that Edwin Pennell was not playing then. In reply PC Horler stated that Norris had been acting as a lookout for the card players. The magistrates were not impressed by the witnesses for the defence and considered the case to be clear against all the defendants who were each find 5s and 2s costs, with the option of seven days in gaol.

The court, however was not finished with Edwin Pennell, Charles Dodge, and the look out, Alfred Norris. They were brought back charged with using obscene language near Dodham Bridge on Sunday, 12 October 1890. PC Horler stated that he had been a short distance away from the defendants when they were hanging about in Gas House Lane and he had written down on a piece of paper the language they had used. He then repeated the expressions which, according to the journalist reporting the proceedings, were of the filthiest nature. Mr Tucker at the Gas Works had overheard the language and had told the defendants that it was abominable. The mayor who was chairman of the magistrates stated that it was very sad to know that they had boys of such a character in the town, and they were liable to severe penalties, but in the hope that leniency would have a good effect the Bench would only fine each of them 5s plus costs, with the option of seven days' imprisonment.

Sunday, 12 October had indeed turned out to be an expensive Sabbath for young Edwin Pennell and Charles Dodge with a total fine of 10s, plus about half as much again in costs, at a time when a working man's wages were unlikely to be much more than £1 10s per week.

AN OCTOBER STORM

The storm which blew east-north-east down the Bristol Channel early on Wednesday, 26 October 1859 co-incided with a rising high spring tide, and was claimed to have been one of the most destructive to hit Weston-super-Mare for some fifty years. Breaking waves sent spray hundreds of feet into the air as the trail of destruction began at Anchor Head where the tide washed away the wall of Dr Godfrey's property, destroying greenhouses, sheds, a bathing house and a playground. Although the Claremont Hotel was perched on a high rock above the sea, waves severely damaged outbuildings and the contents of the landlord's larder were washed away. The whole of a newly-built wall at the Little Strand extending to Knightstone Road was destroyed and waves swept across the road and over Mr Cox's high boundary wall, depositing boulders and sand on his lawns. The storm reserved its full fury for the inner bay east of Knightstone, where over thirty vessels ranging from yachts to colliers were driven against the pier or into each other and smashed to pieces. A yacht and a sloop crashed into the Esplanade, a sailing trow, laden with timber and helpless, was swept under the wall opposite Victoria Buildings and the crew took to the rigging to save themselves.

Along the coast at Burnham-on-Sea, the steamer *Taliesin* was lying alongside the pier, when the schooner *Caroline* was blown across her moorings, snapped them, and the steamer was driven aground; the schooner crashed into the upper part of the pier. The sailing trow *Exeter* ran onto a mud bank where she remained pounded by the raging surf while her crew scrambled up into the rigging to wait until the tide dropped sufficiently for them to be rescued.

In nearby Highbridge, one the the chimneys of Anning's Hotel was blown down and broke through the roof, falling into the bedroom underneath occupied by a Mr Miles. Had it not been for a roof beam under the chimney and immediately over his bed, Mr Miles would have been killed. The gable end of a row of cottages being built by Mr James Cox near the railway was blown down taking part of the roof with it.

In the far west of the county, trees in Dunster Park were felled by the storm and the road between Minehead and Carhampton was blocked by over a score of trees. The passengers in the Taunton coach took refuge in the Luttrell Arms Hotel in Dunster after a hazardous journey across the Park.

The driver of Mr Brice's bread cart from Williton had a miraculous escape when trees fell to the front and back of his vehicle, leaving him and his horses trapped but uninjured. Seventy sheep were drowned at Porlock when huge seas broke over the beach and into the meadows beyond and at Blue Anchor, seven valuable horses were rescued from a pasture flooded by the sea. Huge waves pounded the quay at Minehead, sending spray high over the houses nestling between the sea wall and North Hill. It was only a matter of time before the great seas broke down the wall, poured across the road and sent three feet of water into the houses. In the harbour there was little protection from the huge waves driven in by the storm and although a number of coasting vessels had sought shelter, several were wrecked because the conditions made it impossible to moor them securely and broken boats and masts were strewn along the shore.

Out in the Bristol Channel, a 250-ton ship bound for Waterford, was overwhelmed so quickly in the raging sea that her crew was lucky to escape. The men, suffering hunger and exposure, were picked up by a coastguard cutter and brought safely to Minehead.

Although the storm caused widespread damage and disruption along the Somerset coast, thankfully there appeared to have been no human fatalities.

RICHARD HEWLETT – UNSUCCESSFUL HIGHWAYMAN

Mr Charles Hardwicke, a prosperous grazier and wool company agent from Hewish, near Congresbury, had made about £450 in a good day's trading at Bristol Market on 21 October, 1830. Before leaving the city, he had taken tea with his father, and set out for home at about six o'clock in the evening carrying the cash in his pocket.

Hardwicke had ridden about 5 miles when he came behind another horseman near Newland's Hatch and wished him goodnight as he passed. The rider, whom Hardwicke did not recognise in the gloom, returned the compliment and then asked if the grazier was travelling far. When Hardwicke replied that his destination was beyond Congresbury, the stranger said that he was going the same way and would be glad of company. The two men, making small talk, rode through Congresbury and about a mile or so beyond the village began to cross a lonely stretch of country known as The Heath. The stranger had dropped back a little, when suddenly there was a loud bang and Hardwicke felt a violent blow on his left shoulder. Shouting, 'What was that! Good God what have you done!' he turned in time to see a flash of light. With the same his companion hauled his horse around and rode off at full gallop back along the road they had travelled. Recovering quickly, Hardwicke set out in pursuit shouting, 'Stop him! Stop him!' and finally caught up with his assailant just beyond the bridge over the River Yeo at Congresbury.

As the two men passed a cart left at the side of the road, their horses collided and fell throwing their riders to the ground. Hardwicke scrambled to his feet but as he grappled with his powerful opponent he felt a sharp pain in his left side and then, stunned by several heavy blows to his head, let go. The stranger, thus released remounted, but before he could ride off, Hardwicke recovered sufficiently to grab the horse's bridle and hang on despite being punched about his head. The sound of the struggle brought several local men running to the scene who, having been told by Hardwicke that he had been shot, secured the stranger and took him to the the Ship Aground Inn.

Lukins, the parish constable, was called and the stranger was identified as Richard Hewlett who had farmed at Wick St Lawrence, near Weston-super-Mare. Having been accused of horse stealing some years before, Hewlett had been given £50 by a relative to go to America where it was thought he was still living. A search of his person produced some pistol balls, flints and powder, a map of England and Wales, a book of roads and fairs, a pocket knife and a razor. One of the villagers recovered a lead-weighted swordstick with a bent and blooded 8-inch blade from the scene of the struggle while another had noticed Hewlett throw something into the river as he was taken over the bridge to the inn. A search of the river bed the following morning produced two pistols bound together, one of which had been fired while the flintlock of the second had fallen. However, only the priming in the pan had flashed and the ball and sodden powder still remained undischarged in the barrel; the misfire of the second pistol had no doubt saved the grazier's life.

A surgeon was called to attend Hardwicke who was found to have been shot at close range but the pistol ball was lodged too deep in his left shoulder to be removed. He had also been stabbed in the left side and for over a fortnight lay at the Ship Aground Inn too ill to be moved. At the time of Hewlett's trial, six months later, the court was told that it was doubtful whether Hardwicke would recover the use of his left arm.

Richard Hewlett appeared before Mr Justice Park at the Assizes in Taunton on 2 April 1831 and after a trial lasting nearly seven hours was found guilty of the attempted murder of Mr Charles Hardwicke, and sentenced to death.

The execution took place at Ilchester Gaol on 19 April and the *Western Flying Post* recorded that:

The wretched criminal suffered the full penalty of his crime at Ilchester on Wednesday last. His hopes of a respite which had been entertained up to the latest hour – even to the arrival of the mail – were doomed to meet with disappointment; and on it being communicated that his fate was sealed – that there was no escape from the extreme sentence of the law – his spirits seemed to fail him, and he solicited Mr Hardy, the gaoler, to favour him with a glass of wine which request obtained an immediate compliance. At the prisoner's desire he was attended by Mr Jukes, a dissenting minister of Yeovil. He made no confession of his guilt but intimated that there were circumstances connected with this affair which would not be divulged. He assured Mr Jukes that infidelity had been the cause of his misconduct, but within the last ten months a perusal of Bishop Watson's Apology for the Bible had changed his opinion, though it had not turned him from the path of wickedness. About twenty minutes after eleven o'clock the procession moved towards the place of execution. The executioner preceded the prisoner who was followed by the Revd Messrs Valentine and Jukes, the Under-Sheriff, and Mr Hardy. The miserable man passed along with a firm step, his countenance was pale as death, but it bore a determined and unprepossessing appearance. On passing the prisoners in the court, he turned as if wishing to speak, but walked on without doing so. Having arrived at the drop, he shook hands with those who followed him and then knelt and appeared to pray fervently with Mr Jukes, who at his request addressed the spectators and desired that they would take warning by the present example. The prisoner desired that a little time might be allowed him and after the expiration of a few seconds when everything was adjusted he resolutely threw the handkerchief from him, and was launched fearfully – awfully – into eternity. His struggles could scarcely be observed and to those who were near him they appeared to continue for about five minutes – the body remained the usual time and was then cut down and buried the same evening.

LOVE THY NEIGHBOUR?

The Fidos and the Meads were, to say the least, not on the best of terms in the picturesque village of High Ham overlooking the Somerset Levels. Matters finally came to a head in the main street of Langport on 14 November 1902, and eight weeks later the protagonists found themselves in front of the Somerton Magistrates.

On 5 January 1903, labourer William Fido appeared, summoned for assaulting and beating Mrs Rose Mead at Langport. The Bench was told that ever since Mrs Mead had remonstrated with Mrs Fido about some fowls which had strayed on to her ground, the Fidos had subjected the Meads to abuse and annoyance. Rose Mead told the magistrates 'in a tremulous voice' that on the 14 November last she had been getting into her cart outside a shop in Langport when William Fido came up and waving a stick at her had shouted, 'As for you, I'll do for you if I could, you lady bulldog!' She went on to say that William Fido had threatened her with this 'expression' on several previous occasions, and since that day in Langport she had not dared to leave her home if the defendant were near; she was in terror of her life for fear she might meet him!

The clerk to the magistrates felt obliged to point out that no evidence of battery had been presented by Mrs Mead but Mr Jacks, her solicitor, asked for the defendant to be bound over to keep the peace towards his client. Mr Clarke, representing William Fido, would have none of this and retorted that his client contended that 'the boot was on the other leg', and that his family had suffered annoyance from the Meads. The magistrates expressed the opinion that they were minded to dismiss the case but Mr Jacks appealed to them to bind over the defendant because of his threats and Mr Clarke continued to protest that his client had in no way molested Mrs Mead.

Rose Mead's husband now intervened and shouted that if the Bench did nothing, he would take the law into his own hands as sure as the defendant's name was Fido! Concerned at this outburst, the magistrates retired for a private consultation, and on their return stated that if Mr Jacks could prove any aggressive actions by the defendant since 14 November they would hear it. Mr Mead was put on the stand and stated that William Fido passed his house several times each day in the course of his work and on every occasion he would shout abuse and bad language towards his family. Sometimes the swearing was so bad that Mr Mead could 'not believe that a human being could use such language.' Mr Clarke still contended that there was not sufficient cause to justify his client being bound over, and went on to suggest that the complaints against his client were complete fabrications because the Meads had failed to get William Fido out of his cottage. The solicitor added that the defendant had made a prior complaint to the police that the Meads were molesting him!

The magistrates took the simplest way out of the dilemma and bound over the Fidos and the Meads to keep the peace for six months.

THE MAYOR FLIES TO BRISTOL

The Mayor of Yeovil, Alderman Mitchelmore, had a problem on Tuesday, 24 May 1921. He wanted to visit Bristol during the afternoon but be back in Yeovil for an important meeting in the early evening. Because he could not leave until after lunch it would be very difficult, if not impossible, to get to Bristol and back in the time allowed by road or rail. However, joint managing director of Westland Aircraft and fellow alderman, Percy Petter, came to the rescue by offering to fly the mayor to his appointment in the company's Westland Limousine and bring him back for the evening meeting.

The offer was accepted and, accompanied by Percy Petter and a reporter from a local paper, the mayor boarded the single-engined, three-passenger biplane at 1.30pm on the day in question and with Captain A.S. Keep MC at the controls, the Limousine took off from Westland airfield in beautiful weather.

For Alderman Mitchelmore and the journalist this was their first flight but any 'dubious feelings which might have been entertained beforehand' by the two novice flyers 'were soon set at rest by the remarkable smoothness by which the ascent was made and the wonderful evenness of motion as the flight progressed.' Indeed our correspondent was relieved at not having to negotiate roads of the poor condition of the one going to East Coker or to worry about meeting other motorists at concealed bends and he felt safer than on a recent motor trip to West Dorset.

The flight in the well-lit and upholstered three-seat cabin was described as more like 'floating than flying' as they were 'hurtled through space at a height of 2000 feet at 90 miles an hour surveying the glorious panorama beneath and without suffering the slightest inconvenience.' Half an hour after take-off the Limousine made an easy landing at Filton and within an hour the party was in the heart of Bristol.

Business transacted, the mayor was soon on his way home, passing low over Yeovil to view the Kingston Housing Scheme which was under construction before landing at 5.15pm 'deeply impressed with a wonderful flight and the possibilities of commercial aviation.'

In an exclusive interview after the flight Alderman Mitchelmore recorded his impressions and felt that this was the most comfortable form of locomotion he had tried and that flying left nothing to be desired. The Alderman went on to say, somewhat lyrically, that the view from the air almost 'makes it possible to forget such things as coal strikes, slum cottages and slum areas.' He believed that the interest of Yeovil had 'been so greatly taken up in the consideration of social and industrial problems since the War that the people of our town are in danger of forgetting its great possiblities as a centre of civil aviation.' The mayor expressed the hope that the day would not be too far distant when a trip in an aeroplane would be 'entered upon as commonly as today we enter upon a railway journey and we must hope that Yeovil will be as important a junction as it is today.'

Alderman Petter, the enthusiastic and optomistic plane-maker, believed that the future of civil aviation was assured and the aeroplane was a swift and safe means of travel. There was he explained 'less mechanism in an aeroplane than in a motor car and flights have already been accomplished on a consumption rate of thirty miles to one gallon of petrol. In the air there is a straight road to everywhere and no immediate danger of overcrowding.' No doubt the townsfolk of Yeovil breathed a collective sigh of relief at the mayor's safe return!

THE FATAL FIRING

There was great rejoicing in Langport on the morning of Thursday, 2 August 1866. Margaret, the second daughter of the prominent merchant and shipowner, Edward Bagehot, was marrying George Porch, a banker, from Glastonbury.

Some Langport boatmen and their friends had been given permission to celebrate the occasion by firing salutes from an old six-pounder cannon belonging to Messrs Bagehot & Co. The gun was set up in the company's coal yard on the bank of the River Parrett, and was manned by boatman George Davidge, Walter Webb, a former Royal Marine and now Armoury Sergeant of the 21st Somerset Rifle Volunteers, Sergeant Grimes, the Rifle Volunteers' drill instructor, and boatman, Robert Beck, who was also a veteran Royal Marine.

Walter Webb had command of the gun, and Sergeant Grimes was responsible for preparing the powder charges and placing them in the mouth of the barrel for Webb and Davidge to ram home. There was no proper rammer to clear and sponge out the barrel after each discharge, so the men improvised with a length of wood and a piece of sacking in place of the sponge.

Sergeant Grimes filled three tins with gunpowder and placed them in the barrel, followed by some paper and old clothes to form the wadding and the charge was rammed home by Webb and Davidge. The vent of the cannon was primed by Robert Beck, the slow match applied, and to the delight of the townspeople crowding the coal yard and the river bridge, the gun went off with a flash, an almighty bang and a cloud of smoke billowed across the Parrett.

By one o'clock in the afternoon, three salutes had been fired but as Walter Webb and George Davidge rammed home the charges for the fourth, the cannon went off! Webb's arms were blasted away close to the elbows, his shirt blown to tatters and he was hurled unconscious into the river, followed by Davidge who lost an arm and a hand besides receiving severe gashes to his throat and face. Sergeant Grimes' face was badly scorched, and Beck lost part of the thumb he had placed over the vent to seal it during the loading. A number of spectators standing in the vicinity were slightly injured from the muzzle blast.

Despite his appalling injuries, George Davidge managed to haul himself out of the river and lay bleeding on the bank. Ignoring his burns, Sergeant Grimes leapt into the water and pulled the unconscious Walter Webb up the bank. The two terribly-injured men were carried from the scene, Davidge to his home but, because of his condition, Webb was carried the short distance to the Dolphin Inn where he died five hours later despite the efforts of all the town's medical men to save him. It was reported that the dying man asked to the buried with military honours.

The coroner, Edward Bagehot, held the inquest into Walter Webb's death in the town hall at Langport during the afternoon of the following day. Sergeant Grimes, his face heavily bandaged, was the first witness, and described the events leading up to the cannon's fatal discharge. He explained that both Webb and Davidge appeared to know how to manage the gun and the vent was properly stopped by the veteran Royal Marine, Robert Beck. In reply to a juryman's question, the sergeant thought that some burning rag had been left in the barrel following the previous discharge and that this had been the cause of the explosion.

Robert Beck, the next witness, stated that he had reminded Walter Webb to wet sponge the barrel after the third discharge but this advice had been ignored and the powder rammed home. If the sponging had been done properly, the accident would not have occurred and he considered Walter Webb ought to have known how to manage the gun.

Innkeeper, James Holly, was called, and stated that he had supplied some drink to the men firing the cannon and stayed to watch. He had been standing near the gun and had been knocked over by the force of the fatal discharge. Holly concluded by saying that the firing party were perfectly sober. The inquest jury returned a verdict of accidental death and expressed the hope that the gun would not be used again; they gave their fees to Walter Webb's widow.

The veteran Royal Marine was buried in Huish Episcopi churchyard on Saturday, 4 August 1866, and a firing party from the 21st Somerset Rifle Volunteers fired three volleys over the grave. As Walter Webb was being taken to his final resting place, George Davidge succumbed to his terrible injuries.

EIGHT ESCAPE
FROM PLYMOUTH

In 1823 eight desperate soldiers on the brig *Louisa* were about to leave Plymouth Sound for the fever-ridden west coast of Africa known as the 'white man's grave'. They were part of a punishment detail and they knew their chances of seeing Old England again were pretty slim. It was now or never and, seizing their last opportunity, the eight piled into a boat left unattended alongside the brig and rowed for the shore. Their escape did not go unnoticed and they came under fire from the *Louisa's* guns. Several boats from the tender *Caltiope*, moored nearby, set off in pursuit but the fugitives made the shore and escaped, at least for the time being.

The *Western Flying Post* now takes up the story on 3 February 1823:

A soldier, who was generally called Thomas Thompson, but whose real name was John Higgins, one of the men who escaped from the brig *Louisa*, lying in the Sound at Plymouth, bound for the coast of Africa, under punishment, was apprehended at Chard and has since been committed to Ilchester Gaol. It appears from his account, that being on duty about eight o'clock on the evening of his escape he, with seven others took advantage of a boat having been left alongside, and immediately proceeded to the opposite side of the Sound, where they landed and with much difficulty ascended a steep rock; they then separated. When Thompson arrived at Chard he was accosted by three constables, who asked him to what regiment he belonged, and on his answering to the marines, he was suffered to depart; he, however, lodged there for the night, and the next morning, on his going to a shop kept by Mr Wellington, to purchase some articles for breakfast, his appearance excited the suspicion of Mr W., who asked him to what regiment he belonged; Thompson returned the same answer as he had to the constables; but on inspecting the buttons of his regimental coat and finding his statement to be untrue, Mr W. immediately apprehended him.

The *Western Flying Post* remained silent on the fate of John Higgins, alias Thomas Thompson, and his fellow fugitives.

ARSENIC AND CANDY – A MYSTERY

In the high summer of 1855 the quiet hamlet of Clapton, near Midsomer Norton, was thrown into a great consternation by the sudden death on Friday, 3 August of Emma, the young wife of William Candy, a respectable farmer, and the verdict of the inquest which followed kept the tongues wagging for months.

Twenty-seven-year-old Emma Candy had fallen ill on Thursday, 2 August with violent stomach pains and sickness. Her illness did not give concern until the following evening when suddenly, after complaining of great pain in her 'bowels', her condition rapidly deteriorated and she died before medical assistance could be called. Because of the suddenness of her death, together with some threats she had made to end her life and gossip about another young woman, the coroner, Mr Bruges Fry, decided to hold the inquest.

On Monday, 13 August 1855, the inquest opened and first to give evidence was Emma's husband, William, who stated that they had been married for four years and had a small child. For some time his wife had been in a low state of mind and was often sick, bringing up blood; she had also threatened to kill herself more than once. William Candy said that now and again he had gone out driving with their dairy maid, Miss Huntley, but his wife had not objected and to his knowledge she was not jealous; indeed she had wished him to do so. He went on to say that on the day his wife had died, Mary Swift, their domestic servant, had told him that her mistress had sent her to Midsomer Norton to buy three-pennyworth of powder to kill mice but the girl did not know what had been done with it.

The next witness was Mary Ann Swift who recalled that the day before she died her mistress had been very sick and had brought up some yellow stuff. She had also complained of feeling very thirsty and was drinking all the time. Mary stated that on the Monday morning before she died her mistress had been alone in her bedroom and the servant had overheard her muttering that she would hang or destroy herself. The witness then disclosed that before the inquest Miss Huntley had told her to say that she had never heard her master and mistress quarrel and she was quite willing to say so because she had never heard the couple have bad words. Mr Candy and Miss Huntley were fond of each other because they were cousins but she had never heard her mistress complain about the friendship.

Mary Swift recounted how, about a week before Mrs Candy died, she had been sent to Mr Dudden's shop in Midsomer Norton to buy rat poison but she did not know what her mistress had done with it. She knew that Mr Candy kept poison to kill mice in the barn and house but she had not questioned why her mistress wanted some. There were gasps as the witness told of an occasion when Mrs Candy had been very upset, and how she had stopped her from cutting her throat. On mentioning this to a servant who had once worked for the household, she was told that Mrs Candy had trouble and she would soon find out what it was. Mary stated that she had asked her mistress the cause of the trouble but she would never tell.

Jane Whittuck, a needlewoman who occasionally worked for the family, testified that Mrs Candy had told her that she would take arsenic if she could get some but had then instructed the witness not say anything to her husband. The needlewoman said that she had seen Mr Candy driving out with Miss Huntley but she had never heard any quarrels about it.

Neighbour Thomas Batt stated that during the previous November Mr Candy had sent for him and told him that he had just restrained Emma from killing herself. When the witness asked why she should wish to destroy herself, William Candy had said that his wife had a religious impression that her soul was lost and there was no mercy for her. Thomas Batt stated that Emma had been present in the room when this was being said and did not contradict her husband.

The coroner adjourned the inquest until 20 August and asked the press to refrain from disclosing the evidence until after the adjournment. Although the newspapers kept silent on the details of the proceedings on 15 August the *Taunton Courier* reported that 'there being no doubt that the deceased's death was the result of poison, the question for the jury to decided will be whether it was by her own hand or that of another.' Local people had been at the inquest and the picture which they saw emerging, and no doubt gossiped about, was one of possible infidelity, suicide, and perhaps something more sinister.

The first witness at the adjourned inquest was Mr Robert Boodle, surgeon, from neighbouring Chilcompton, who had carried out the post-mortem examination of Emma Candy. He stated that death was due to inflammation of the stomach and intestines caused, he believed, by an acrid poison. He had therefore placed the stomach with its contents and the intestines in jars which he sealed and immediately despatched to Bristol for examination by Mr William Herapath, the analytical chemist renowned for his forensic expertise.

The next witness was the chemist, Mr Herapath, who stated that the stomach was highly inflamed but not ulcerated, and the contents consisted principally of curdled milk in which he had found a considerable quantity of arsenic. He had no doubt that death had been caused by white arsenious acid which he believed had been taken in milk. Mr Herapath stated that he had also received from Mr Boodle a small package labelled 'Butler Vermin and Insect Killer – Poison' which he found to contain a large portion of arsenic, a small portion of carbonate and a little dark coloured powder. If the Butler's mixture had been taken into the stomach the chemist believed that the dark powder would have discoloured the milk curd but he had found no such discolouration. Having established the cause of death he had not gone on to examine the deceased's intestines and therefore could not confirm that signs of the powder were not present in these organs. Mr Herapath went on to explain that if the arsenic had been taken at one time and the milk at another, he would not have expected to find so much arsenic combined with the curd and therefore, in his opinion, the arsenic was taken with the milk. Although he could not say how much poison had been taken, the quantity he found was sufficient to penetrate the woman's system and cause her death. Because the milk curd had not been digested, the chemist believed that the arsenic had been taken shortly before Emma Candy died. Mr Herapath then graphically described the common symptoms of poisoning by arsenic. The victim would suffer violent sickness and diarrhoea, there would be a burning sensation in the stomach and intestines, frequent cramps, loss of strength and great agony up to the time of death. In his experience, a person dying from arsenic poisoning 'must necessarily indicate to those about him his state of intense agony.'

At this point, Mr W.C. Cruttwell, William Candy's solicitor, intervened and asked the chemist to elaborate on his examination of the deceased's stomach. Mr Herapath explained that there was more arsenic in the curd than he would have expected from the small quantity of solid arsenic remaining in the stomach. Following the administration of arsenic, the pains usually came on about six hours later and death would occur within twenty-four hours.

The coroner then asked the witness whether alcohol had played any part in the death of Mrs Candy? Mr Herapath replied that he did not believe so, but as he had not been looking for its presence he could not say whether there was any alcohol in the stomach. Mr Boodle, the surgeon, was recalled, and stated that if the deceased had drunk alcohol shortly before she died he would have smelt it during the post-mortem examination but apart from a slight vinous odour, there was no smell of spiritous liquor.

Mr Richard Dudden, the druggist of Midsomer Norton, stated that he had a vague recollection of a young woman similar to Mary Ann Swift purchasing three-pennyworth of Butler's Vermin and Insect Killer from his shop towards the end of July. He had sold no pure arsenic within the past month. He explained that under the Arsenic Act he was forbidden to sell the poison to persons whom he did not know unless it was coloured with soot or indigo dye and because Butler's powder was so coloured he had sold it to the servant.

Mary Ann Swift was recalled but stated that she could not recollect who sold her the powder. She had never been to the shop before and would not know the person again if she saw him. The coroner then asked Mary to describe her mistress's final days. The servant stated that Mrs Candy had been ill the day before she died and Mr Bourne had attended on the Thursday afternoon but the medicine he had given her had made her sick. Miss Huntley had been in the room most of the time and had slept with Mrs Candy the night before she died; she had noticed no coolness between her mistress and Miss Huntley and they appeared to be on the best of terms. Mary Swift stated that milk was taken up to Mrs Candy every morning and she recollected taking some from the cheese tub to her mistress the day before she died. Miss Huntley had told her that at the sick woman's request she had given her a glass of raw gin before breakfast on the day she died, followed by rum and water and a glass of porter. The witness stated that besides herself, the only persons in the house when Mrs Candy died, were her husband, child and Miss Huntley.

The next witness was the Candy's medical practitioner, Mr Thomas Bourne, a surgeon from Radstock. He recollected that on the afternoon of Thursday, 2 August he had been called to see Mrs Candy and found her in bed. She had told him that she had been very sick and had brought up blood. Although the sickness had stopped and the patient seemed much easier, she complained of having had very severe stomach pain and of feeling very thirsty. Having satisfied himself that there was no apparent inflammation of the stomach and her breathing was natural, Mr Bourne ordered Mrs Candy to remain in bed and said that he would call again on Saturday; in the meantime he would send over some medicine. On his return home the surgeon made up a mixture of one drachm of carbonate of soda, twenty-four grains of nitrate of potash, six drops of prussic acid, half a drachm of tincture of cardamoms and water, eight pills containing one gram of acetate of morphine and eight grains of extract of hop, and some powders each containing five grains of tartaric acid. The medicine was sent over to the patient with instructions for a mustard plaster to be applied to her stomach soon after the mixture was taken if she did not seem any better. Mr Bourne stated that he had not believed Mrs Candy's condition to be dangerous but before he left he had told her husband and Miss Huntley that the patient should only eat gruel or arrowroot and on no account should she have any strong drink. The surgeon recollected that when he had examined the patient on the Thursday afternoon he felt certain that she had not taken poison but was suffering from inflammation of the stomach, an old complaint for which he had treated her in the past. When he had spoken to Mr Candy following the death of his wife, he was told that she had taken only one of the pills and then drunk some porter, followed the next day by gin and rum. The surgeon stated that he had been most concerned that his instructions had been ignored but when he had remonstrated with Mr Candy, telling him that these things were sufficient to kill his wife, he had replied that she had insisted on drinking the liquors. Mr Bourne stood down and the coroner adjourned the inquest for another week until 27 August.

First to give evidence on the 27th was Mary Ann Saunders who stated that she had been in the service of the deceased for four months until last July when she had been discharged because Mr Candy had told her that they needed only one servant. The witness recollected that on 31 July she had gone to the farm to collect her wages and was told by Mary Swift that Mr Candy was upstairs with Miss Huntley. Mary Saunders disclosed that during the months she had lived at the farm she had seen Mr Candy kiss Miss Huntley in the milk house and Mrs Candy had told her that she had seen her husband and Miss Huntley on the bed together more than once and if she caught them again 'she would make public of it.' Her late mistress seemed to be very troubled and although she had exclaimed several times that she would hang herself, the witness had never heard Mr and Mrs Candy quarrel. Mary Saunders said that Miss Huntley was often poorly and sometimes Mr Candy carried her in her chair to the table.

All eyes were now upon William Candy as he took the stand for a second time. He stated that he had given his wife one of Mr Bourne's pills, some of the mixture and one of the powders each time she had taken it. He could not recall seeing Miss Huntley give his wife any medicine but she had given her some rum and water; he had not given Emma any beer, porter or spiritous liquor. He agreed that Mr Bourne had ordered only gruel and arrowroot to be given to his wife but she had refused it and insisted she must have what her stomach could take. William Candy recollected that during the evening of her death, his wife had complained of great pain in her bowels and of being very warm and thirsty. Towards midnight her breath became short and seeing that she was becoming worse he had sent the farm boy for Mr Bourne and Mrs Maggs, a neighbour. However the boy had returned saying that he could make no one hear and so the lad was sent to call out Mr Steeds, Emma's father, but she died just after he left. During her final hours his wife had said nothing about poisoning herself and neither did she accuse anyone. While it was true that Emma had threatened to kill herself it had never occurred to him that she might have taken poison. His wife had never accused him of paying undue attention to his cousin, Miss Huntley. William Candy stated that when he had informed Mr Bourne that his wife had taken some rum and water, the surgeon had told him that he could not answer for a patient who would not observe his instructions. In reply to a question from the foreman of the jury, William Candy said that besides the rum and water his wife had drunk some porter and gin. When he had told Mr Bourne about this, the surgeon had exclaimed that this was enough to kill her! Questioned by Mr T.W. Saunders, the lawyer acting for Mr Steeds, Emma's father, William Candy stated that his wife had been sick almost immediately after taking her first medicine.

During the Thursday he had been working about the farm and looked in on occasion to see how she was. Emma had been sick several times throughout the day and because she was so unwell, Miss Huntley had remained with his wife and slept with her that night. On the Friday morning he had given Emma some milk and a pill but, although she refused to take another, she had drunk some of the mixture and taken a powder. Leaving Miss Huntley in attendance he had gone haymaking for most of the day. Asked by Mr Saunders whether he kept poison, the farmer confirmed that he occasionally used a mixture to kill insects affecting his sheep and for rats and mice in the barn, but it was locked away in his bureau and he held the key on his person. He had never kept pure arsenic and there was no mixture in the house at the time of his wife's death. Replying to a question from Mr Cruttwell, his solicitor, William Candy said that his wife had a chest of drawers in her room and one drawer was always kept locked. However he did not go on to say whether it had been opened and anything suspicious found after her death. Questioned about the milk he had given to his wife on the Friday morning, Candy stated that it had been taken from the cheese tub and shortly afterwards the contents of the tub were made into cheese.

One of the jurors enquired how often Emma Candy had been sick and William Candy recollected that she was sick on the Thursday morning before Mr Bourne had seen her and most mornings during the previous few weeks. Asked by the Coroner whether his wife had been in the family way, William Candy replied that he did not know.

Jane Whittuck was recalled and strongly denied rumours that money had been given to her to withhold evidence. Questioned further, she agreed that she had spoken to Mary Ann Saunders and had suggested that when she was talking about Mrs Candy, if she did not know anything about 'the matter' she had no need to say anything. Miss Huntley had never offered the witness a new gown to 'keep dark' on the subject.

Mary Ann Saunders was recalled and testified that Jane Whittuck had come to her house on the Sunday following Mrs Candy's death and asked her if she had seen 'anything.' When she replied that she had seen very little, Jane Whittuck had said that if this was so it was not worthwhile mentioning it. The needlewoman had not promised her anything or said that it would be better for her to say nothing.

Mary Ann Swift was recalled and disclosed that Miss Huntley had given her a dress on the Saturday week following her mistress's death but had said nothing more than 'There's a dress for you. I am going away.' Miss Huntley had given her no money or anything else but Mr Candy had given her a black frock on the day of the funeral. No one had promised to raise her wages since her mistress had died.

Mary Ann Swift was the last witness and, following the coroner's summing-up, the jury held a brief consultation and returned their verdict finding that 'The deceased Emma Candy died from swallowing a quantity of arsenic, but by whom given we have no evidence to prove.' The two lawyers, Mr Cruttwell and Mr Saunders, thanked Mr Bruges Fry for the impartial and able manner in which he had conducted the investigation and the proceedings terminated.

The verdict provided much for the gossips to chew over. What had happened to the rat poison bought for Emma Candy and what was in the locked drawer in her room? Was there infidelity and were some witnesses put under pressure? Where was Miss Huntley and why did she not appear as a witness at the inquest? Did Emma Candy kill herself in a most agonizing way or was she taking small doses of arsenic to make herself ill and thereby attract her husband's attention away from Miss Huntley but took a fatal dose by mistake? Or was there something more sinister at work?

THE TRAGEDY ON
THE WEYMOUTH EXCURSION

On Friday, 8 August 1913 the Great Western Railway Company's record-breaking locomotive, the 'City of Bath', drawing the Paddington to Weymouth express, slowed down as it approached the bend into Yeovil Pen Mill station but, as it passed the north signal box, Driver Thomas Dowler and his fireman, Richard Carver, were puzzled to see the signalman pointing frantically towards the front of their engine. In the moment while they peered forward to see what was wrong they missed the starter signal which still stood at danger and then, to Driver Dowler's horror, he saw, only an engine length away, the rear carriages of the London to Weymouth excursion train standing in the station. Frantically he applied the brakes but, although his train was travelling at less than walking pace, it was too late and the City of Bath ploughed like a remorseless piston into the last carriage, crushing and compressing the six compartments into a mass of splintered wood and twisted metal.

In the last carriage of the excursion, passengers for Yeovil were wondering how long it would be before the train was drawn forward to the platform so that they could get out, and others were impatient to be on their way; they were already half an hour late.

Mrs Louisa Redmond was fearful of missing the Pen Mill to Taunton connection for if she did her husband, Harry, would have a long wait for her at Durston station. Harry Redmond, a sewerman from Paddington, had been spending a week's holiday with Louisa's family and she planned to spend the weekend with him before the couple returned to London. In one of the compartments, three young women were impatient to get out and start their holidays in the beautiful surroundings of Melbury Park. Edith and Emma Groves, the daughters of the park lodge keeper, and their cousin, Alice Jenkins, would soon be home and for the next three weeks would be free from the daily routine of their lives in service in London. How much longer would they have to wait – they had already been on the train for over three hours! Also impatient to be on their way to Weymouth and a week's holiday were Joshua Blythe and his fiancee, Minnie Fryer. Mrs Jane Legg had been looking forward to sitting down to a late tea with her husband and family at Stover Court in St Michael's Lane, Bridport, but now it was beginning to look more like supper.

The Friday evening suddenly disintegrated into a horror of crashing, rending and tearing of wood and metal; then silence.

Recovering from the shock, the station staff rushed to the scene and were horrified to see the great steam engine buried in the smashed carriage. Helped by passengers from the excursion train, they began to tear at the wreckage and several people, some miraculously uninjured, were quickly released. Then Mrs Louisa Redmond was brought out, dead, crushed by the wreckage, but it was another hour before the next casualty could be extracted. This was young Hilda Barrett, from East Ham, who was alive but very badly bruised. Trapped next to Hilda was a dazed Frank Waters who seemed to be unhurt, but a closer examination revealed both legs to be fractured and his left hip dislocated. He was gently removed and, with Hilda, was quickly conveyed to hospital.

During the time the rescuers were working they could see Emma Groves trapped in the wreckage but they could do nothing for her until Hilda and Frank were released. Emma's life had been saved by cushions shielding her head, but she was desperately injured with both legs terribly crushed – they would be amputated shortly after her admission to hospital. It took another twenty minutes to release Emma but when the rescue team reached the silent form of a woman they could see beneath her they found Jane Legg dead.

Joshua Blythe was brought out with a broken leg but Minnie, his bride to be, escaped with severe bruising. They would spend their holiday recovering in Yeovil hospital. Alice Jenkins was badly bruised but her cousin, Edith Groves, was badly injured with a compound fracture of her left leg and the right completely shattered. One of the last passengers to be released, and the eighth injured, was Raymond Newman from Camberwell who, within a few days, would lose his severely crushed right leg.

There were stories of miraculous escapes from death or injury in the tangled wreckage. Six passengers in the middle compartment were thrown onto the floor but saved from injury or worse, by the seats and cushions forming a protective arch. A mother and her two small children were also trapped but amazingly they had escaped injury, and as rescuers removed the tangle of metal and wood around them, the mother insisted that the two children be taken out before any attempt was made to release her.

Two passengers were dead and eight injured and although the small Yeovil hospital was almost overwhelmed by the casualties and the severity of some of the injuries, the doctors and staff coped magnificently, so that within the next few days it could be reported that all, but Edith Groves, were on their way to recovery.

In the aftermath of the crash, the inquest opened on the following Monday in Yeovil Town Hall where the jury heard how the excursion was half an hour late; how the last carriage overlapped the platform so that the passengers could not alight until the train was pulled forward; how there was a delay in bringing the carriage to the platform because a milk van had to be taken off the front of the excursion and shunted into a siding; how there was a delay in shunting the excursion from the main line to allow the express through; how the signalman had correctly taken the express through the several sections on the approach to the station but suddenly becoming aware that the speed of the train would take it through the last signal, set at danger, had tried to attract the driver's attention to the excursion; how the driver and fireman said that they had been distracted as they passed the signal box and had missed the vital signal; that the speed of the express had been slowed to a walking pace or less; that if the visibility on the bend had not been obstructed by high wagons standing in a siding, the driver of the express would have seen the excursion standing in the station from a much greater distance, and would have been able to stop in time.

A verdict of death by misadventure was reached on the two women who, sadly, would be joined by a third before the week was out. Poor Edith Groves never recovered from her terrible injuries and gave up the fight for life on 15 August. The local newspaper reported that her coffin was conveyed in a glass-sided hearse to the quiet churchyard in Melbury Osmond, a far different home-coming to that imagined by the unfortunate young girl when she had started out in such high spirits for her holiday less than a fortnight before.

The Board of Trade Inspector who conducted the official inquiry into the crash found that Driver Dowler had allowed his train to pass the signal set at danger and concluded that 'the responsibility for this accident must, therefore, rest mainly on him.' The inspector also commented that the arrangements at Pen Mill Station could not be regarded as entirely satisfactory because the platforms were not long enough to accommodate the length of the trains using them. Owing to the curvature of the lines, the driver of a down train could not get a good view of the line in front of him when he was entering the station. He considered it desirable that the scheme, which the Great Western Railway Company had for remodelling the station, including the lengthening of the platforms, should be started soon.

SOMETHING IN THE ATTIC

Albert Dyer climbed the narrow rickety staircase into the attics of the old mansion house known as The Green in Broad Street at Somerton and placed the length of gas pipe on the dusty floor. It was nearly five o'clock and once he had lifted up the floor boards and laid the pipe ready for connection he would go home to tea.

The renovation of The Green, which was situated just off the main street on the north side of the church, was going well but much work was still needed as very little had been done by Mr Thomas Welsh who had lived there for most of his eighty years. The old man had died the year before and the new owner, Mr E.W. Valentine, was carrying out fairly extensive work on the property.

Albert thought that he might come back after tea as there would still be light enough for a few more hours work in the evening of 31 August 1896. He removed one of the floorboards and then opened the door to a recess cupboard in the wall to continue the line of the pipe. Here the boards were loose and, on lifting the first one, the workman was startled to see a little skeleton lying in the space between the cupboard floor and the ceiling of the room below. Scrambling back down the attic stairs he sent for Mr Valentine who hurried to the house with Dr Wade. The skeleton was carefully taken out and, when several adjoining floor boards were lifted, three more bundles were found lying side by side. On being removed and unwrapped each revealed the small bones of an infant. Police Sergeant Comer was summoned and the four pathetic bundles of bone were taken to the police station where Dr Wade made a detailed examination.

The news of the gruesome find quickly spread through the town and the gossip began. Old Mr Welsh had been a bachelor of 'rather eccentric habits' and, during the last thirty years of his life, a single woman going by the name of Eliza 'the Queen' Edwards (her true surname was Martin), had been his resident housekeeper. When he died the old man had left her a cottage and £100 a year to live on. The fifty-year-old former housekeeper now shared the cottage with her married son, but because her mind was 'somewhat deranged' she had not been told of the discovery. However the tongues were wagging and there was much speculation about the parentage of the four infants.

The inquest was held a week later in Somerton Court House and after the jury had viewed the bones the coroner formally opened the proceedings. He stated that without doubt the four infants had been deliberately concealed under the floorboards but whether they had been born alive was a matter for speculation. Albert Dyer testified to finding the skeletons and he was followed by Dr Wade who described their condition. He stated that most of the flesh had gone from the bones and he could not establish the sex of each infant or how it had died. Two appeared to have been fully-developed new-born infants and the other two were probably premature. The fully-developed infants could have been born alive but there were no signs to prove this. It was impossible to say how long the bodies had been under the floorboards; it could have been anything from five to twenty years and perhaps even more.

Police Sergeant Comer told how he had gone to the house and taken the skeletons back to the police station where he made a thorough examination of the material in which three of them were wrapped. One was wrapped in what appeared to be a child's napkin tied round with tape, the second in a piece of bed curtain and the third in an apron and towel. However he could find no identifying marks to indicate ownership of the articles. Sergeant Comer stated that he had thoroughly searched the house and garden but nothing further was found. One of the jurymen remarked that one of the pieces of apron cloth was similar to material made in Somerton and worn in the town about ten years before.

All the witnesses had now given evidence and the coroner stated that the remains should be preserved for an indefinite period and the best place to keep them might be the local museum. The jury returned an open verdict and the police were recommended to keep the cloth wrappings for further examination.

The mystery of the four tiny bodies hidden the attic of The Green was never solved.

THE HOMICIDAL SERVANT GIRL

One of the hidden fears of the employers of servants in the nineteenth century almost came to fruition when fourteen-year-old Elizabeth Vince put something nasty in her mistress's breakfast arrowroot and found herself before Mr Justice Park at the Somerset Spring Assizes in April 1827 charged with administering poison with intent to murder Mrs Tereza Eliza Fry.

Mrs Fry kept a boarding school at Coombe Villa, about two miles from Bath, and in the autumn of 1826, Elizabeth Vince, a pauper girl, was placed in her service by the overseers of the poor of the parish of Walcot.

A few weeks later, some sugar of lead was bought to treat the eyes of a gentleman lodger at Coombe Villa, and one afternoon, Elizabeth brought some to her mistress saying that it was burnt alum for her baby's ulcerated mouth. Horrified, Mrs Fry exclaimed that this was a deadly poison and snatching it from the girl, put it into a packet on which she wrote 'Rank Poison', and locked it away on the top shelf of the cupboard in the breakfast parlour.

On the morning of 4 December, Mrs Fry sat down to breakfast and Elizabeth brought her a basin of arrowroot saying that the cook had left it to her mistress to sweeten it. Noticing what seemed to be water floating on the surface of the porridge-like food she asked why the cook had added water but the girl replied that she had seen it made and only milk had been put in. Mrs Fry took the first spoonful but finding it sweet, enquired why Elizabeth had said that it was unsweetened. She ate another spoonful but now the arrowroot tasted acid, a similar flavour to that of cream of tartar, and the cook was summoned to explain what was going on. Puzzled by the complaint the cook denied adding anything to the arrowroot, indeed she had eaten what had been left in the saucepan and it tasted very good. To prove her point, the cook ate a spoonful from the basin but had to agree that there was an unusual taste. Shortly after both the cook and Mrs Fry were seized with violent stomach cramps and for a while were quite ill. Mrs Fry suspected that all was not well and that someone had tampered with the arrowroot. Going to the cupboard in the breakfast parlour she found the packet containing the sugar of lead was missing and so was a small box of oxalic acid, another very nasty poison used in those days as a bleaching and cleaning agent.

To confirm his wife's suspicions, Mr Fry hastened into Bath with the basin and the remains of the arrowroot which he gave to Mr Day, a surgeon, who confirmed that something had been added and suggested that he should take it to Mr Cuff, a local chemist, for analysis.

Back at Coombe Villa, Elizabeth Vince was being subjected to strict questioning by a now-recovered Mrs Fry, but after vehemently denying adding anything to the arrowroot she accused the cook. Bursting into tears Elizabeth confessed to seeing the cook take something out of a small packet, place it in a cup and then pour some arrowroot on top of it. The cook had then mixed it all together, added some milk, poured it into the saucepan and placed it on the fire to boil. The cook was sent for and Elizabeth repeated her story, adding that she would tell it again on oath. The cook emphatically denied everything, pointing out that she had eaten the arrowroot and suffered the same attack as her mistress.

The questioning of Elizabeth Vince continued and finally she broke down and confessed to taking the two packets from the cupboard and adding the sugar of lead to the arrowroot; the other packet she had thrown away. She was taken before two local magistrates who sent the girl for trial at the next assizes.

The Frys could not understand why Elizabeth acted as she did for they believed that they had treated her with kindness, even though a few small articles had gone missing after she had joined the household. In fact a few days before 4 December Mrs Fry had mentioned the losses to a friend who had suggested a visit to 'the conjuring man' who would show them the guilty person in a glass.

The trial of Elizabeth Vince opened before Mr Justice Park and Mr Gunning, the prosecuting counsel, outlined the events leading up to the charge and then told the judge that there was some doubt whether the basin containing the arrowroot was the same as the one delivered to Surgeon Day. The judge ordered the chemist, Mr Cuff, to the witness box to explain what had happened. The chemist stated that he had analysed the contents of a basin given to him by Mr Fry, but there was no sign of sugar of lead or oxalic acid in the mixture. As the basin had passed through so many hands, it was impossible to identify it and its contents as being the same as that given to Mrs Fry.

On hearing this Mr Justice Park stopped the trial, ruling that it would impossible to arrive at a safe conviction and Elizabeth Vince was acquitted. However the judge had not finished with Elizabeth and told her that after reading the depositions of the witnesses, he had no doubt that she had committed the crime and was a very lucky girl. If it had been proved, and despite her tender age, she would have been sentenced to death as an example to 'deter others from such enormous wickedness.'

MR MORFORD
AND THE GERMAN SPY

Great Britain's declaration of war on Germany was less than ten days old when at about nine o'clock on the evening of 13 August 1914 Lieutenant H.C. Palmer of the London Scottish Rifles drove his car into Shepton Mallet and stopped at the Hare and Hounds for refreshment. Lieutenant Palmer was still recovering from an operation for appendicitis, major surgery in 1914, and had been recalled to his Territorial Regiment in London from three weeks sick leave.

Earlier that evening, the last of the local Territorials mustered for wartime service had left Shepton Mallet and many of the crowd, which had waved them goodbye, were still milling about the town in a state of patriotic fervour, fuelled in some cases by a few drinks. Since war was declared on 4 August the whole nation had been caught up in a surge of patriotism and in the imagination of large numbers of the population there were enemy spies everywhere – a foreign-sounding name, especially a German one, a stranger in town or anything out of the ordinary contributed to the 'Spy craze.' It was into this heated and excited atmosphere that Lieutenant Palmer drove and parked outside the hotel at the junction of Commercial Road and the High Street.

Shortly after entering the hotel, the lieutenant was joined by a gentleman who introduced himself as Mr Rupert Morford, a local veterinary surgeon, and following some initial pleasantries, the officer invited his new acquaintance to join him in a whisky and soda. The discussion turned to the war and, after explaining that he was a Territorial officer under orders to ask questions, Mr Morford began to enquire about Lieutenant Palmer's regiment, his reasons for being in Shepton Mallet and his destination. The officer readily answered the questions and seemed rather amused at the manner of his interrogator who was scribbling in a note book and becoming more excited as the conversation proceeded. Another whisky and soda was ordered and for a while the two were joined by Mr Ozzard, a local journalist.

Duly refreshed and anxious to be away, Lieutenant Palmer and Mr Morford walked out into the street but as they reached the motor car his companion suddenly pushed him into the vehicle shouting, 'Hands up! You'll not leave here tonight!' and waving his notebook in the air exclaimed to the crowd, clustered around the car, 'I've enough to hang him! He's a German spy.' Despite the officer protesting that he was nothing of the sort Mr Morford continued to shout that he had caught a German spy and he would prove it.

Sergeant Fry and Constable Priddle were on duty in the police station in Commercial Road and hearing the noise of the disturbance outside the Hare and Hounds went to investigate. They found a crowd milling around a motor car and an excited Mr Morford standing on the step of the vehicle shouting that he had caught a German spy. On seeing the policeman, the veterinarian called for them to come and read his notes which would hang the spy. Concerned at the state of Mr Morford, Sergeant Fry persuaded him to leave his 'spy' for a moment but suddenly he lashed out with his fists and was only restrained with some difficulty. The sergeant cautioned Mr Morford about his conduct and after being told to go home, otherwise he would be locked up, the veterinarian departed the scene.

Meanwhile the crowd around the motor car had become threatening and it was with some difficulty that Sergeant Fry managed to extract Lieutenant Palmer and take him to the security of the police station. Enquiries by telephone of the officer commanding the London Scottish Rifles established the lieutenant's identity and confirmed that he had been recalled for duty.

Sergeant Fry walked with the officer back to the Hare and Hounds to protect him from the angry crowd which was still shouting that he was a German spy, but found that in his absence two of the motor car's tyres had been punctured and it had been taken into the nearby garage for repair. The sergeant remained in the garage while the tyres were being repaired, but on going outside to investigate an increase in the disturbance in the street found Mr Morford, this time accompanied by his wife and some ladies, standing up in his pony trap once more haranguing the crowd. Going up to the veterinarian, Sergeant Fry advised him to be quiet and go home but he refused. The policeman thereupon turned the horse and trap around and, after leading it away from the crowd, told Mr Morford that this was his last chance and if he did not go home he would be locked up.

The crowd was still milling about outside the garage when Sergeant Fry returned but on going to investigate another outbreak of shouting he found Mr Morford struggling with Constable Priddle who was trying to remove him from the pony trap. The sergeant acted immediately, he arrested Mr Morford and took him to the police station where he was charged with being drunk and was locked up for the night.

Lieutenant Palmer, his motor car repaired, finally left Shepton

Mallet shortly after midnight, and no doubt regaled the officers' mess with the tale of his arrest as a German spy by a drunken veterinary surgeon masquerading as an officer in a small Somerset town.

Mr Rupert Morford appeared before the magistrates on the following morning and pleaded not guilty to being drunk and disorderly. Various witnesses described the events and one expressed the opinion that it had been one of the most disgraceful scenes he had observed in Shepton Mallet for twenty years and Mr Morford was the cause of it. In his defence, Mr Morford stated that after seeing the Territorials off at the railway station he had come back into the town and had been told that there was something unusual about the uniform worn by an officer who had just arrived at the Hare and Hounds. He had approached the officer to find out who he was and, although he had drunk two whisky and sodas with him, he was not drunk. Mr Morford stated that he had pretended to be an officer to draw out replies from the suspect and read some entries from his notebook, one of which commented that the officer's coat looked like a German one. He explained that he had prevented the crowd from overturning the officer's car and strongly denied that he had been drunk and disorderly.

The magistrates were not impressed and Mr Morford was found guilty and fined £2 with 19s 6d costs. As he left the court, Mr Morford remarked that he would not go spy catching again for a little while.

THE PASSING OF
TREVOR HOYLE

The air raid warnings wailed across Yeovil at eleven o'clock on the morning of Wednesday, 26 March 1941 and were the 117th alert since the beginning of the war. People hurried to shelter and waited apprehensively for the characteristic undulating sound of the engines of the German bombers they had heard so many times before.

The children at Huish Infants' School nervously chattered and fidgeted in their air raid shelter alongside the Yeovil Town football field. Five-year-old Trevor Hoyle was in his first year at the school and when the assistant teacher in charge of the shelter told him that he could go home, he no doubt hoped that mummy had come for him. It was, however, not Mrs Lily Hoyle who was waiting for Trevor but he recognised the lady as being one of his mummy's friends and his disappointment was quickly over.

About three quarters of an hour had passed since the alert began and although on many previous occasions a raid had not materialised, the children were not allowed to leave the school before the sirens gave the All Clear; if, however, a parent called the child could go home. The mother explained that she had come to take her daughter home and told the teacher that her friend, Mrs Hoyle, had asked her to collect Trevor as well. She promised to see the little boy to his home at 23 Westland Terrace, close to the Westland Aircraft works and potentially one of the most dangerous areas of Yeovil at the time. Although there had been attacks on the factory, most of the bombs had fallen in the neighbouring residential areas or in the town centre and civilians had been killed and wounded.

Suddenly, at noon, a twin-engine German bomber dived from the clouds and attacked the Westland works with high explosive bombs and sprayed the town with machine gun fire. The majority of the bombs fell in one of the neighbouring residential areas destroying and seriously damaging houses in Westland Terrace. The Hoyle home received a direct hit and was completely destroyed.

As the emergency teams worked amongst the devastation, the news broke that Lily Hoyle and Trevor were missing and this gave urgency to the rescue parties as they set to work to clear the rubble. The bomb had blown the house to pieces and the experienced rescuers knew there was little hope that the mother and son would be found alive. Before long, the remains of a woman's body were found and identified as Lily Hoyle, but despite an extensive search of the remains of the home and the immediate vicinity, no sign of Trevor was found; he had simply disappeared from the face of the earth. Local people were very distressed at the failure to find the little boy and the search was not called off until all were satisfied that there was no hope.

The lone 'hit and run' raider had caused death and injury at Westland Terrace and in the factory for when the All Clear sounded one hour later it was found that seven other people had died and over thirty men and women were wounded.

The police carried out enquiries and established that at least three people had seen a young boy corresponding to Trevor's description walking in Westland Road a few minutes before the bombs fell. One of the air raid wardens on duty in Westland Road saw Trevor walk along the road and turn down the cul-de-sac where he lived. The boy was by himself and the warden recalled that he was wearing a greenish coat. He did not see Trevor again and about ten minutes later the bombs fell. A second warden recalled that at about a quarter to twelve he saw Trevor walk along Westland Road and turn down Westland Terrace. He said that the boy was carrying his gas mask and wearing a green coat; some ten minutes later the bombs dropped. Trevor was also seen in the distance by a neighbour walking alone in Westland Road and she saw him turn into the cul-de-sac to his home. None of the witnesses remembered seeing Trevor with the mother and daughter.

The identity of the mother who collected Trevor from the school remains a mystery. Apparently she did not accompany the boy to his home because the neighbour and the two wardens said that he had been on his own. So what really happened? There is, I think, an explanation to the mystery. It is more than likely that, as an active youngster, Trevor was running on ahead of the mother who was following at a distance and keeping an eye on him as they made their way home. This would explain why the witnesses stated that he was on his own. It is also most probable that the mother was one of the wounded neighbours taken to hospital and was never interviewed by the police.

Mrs Lily Hoyle was buried in Yeovil Cemetery on 3 April 1941, but little Trevor has no grave or monument, only the four winds to which he was consigned in a split second of horror.

A GAOL BREAK FOILED AND A MYSTERY SOLVED, PERHAPS

Arthur Thistlewood was a revolutionary and for his small band of followers, he was a fatally unsuccessful one. Thistlewood had prepared a plan to blow up the British Cabinet during a dinner at the Earl of Harrowby's house on 23 February 1820, seize key buildings in London and declare a revolutionary republic. His small band of thirteen met in a stable loft in Cato Street, off the Edgware Road, and prepared to carry out their plan. The men were heavily armed, but before they could set out on their revolution, soldiers and Bow Street officers raided the loft and, in the brief scuffle, Thistlewood ran one officer through with his sword. The plot had been betrayed by a police informer who had infiltrated the group and the ringleaders were tried for treason, found guilty and executed on 1 May 1820. As traitors the method of their execution was particularly gruesome for after being hung, the bodies were decapitated by a man wearing a black mask and dressed as a sailor. His identity remained a mystery until February seven years later.

On the 8 February 1827 the *Taunton Courier* ran the following story:

Ilchester Gaol. A conspiracy amongst the prisoners confined in this gaol, to break prison, was, we understand, a few days since discovered, and the discovery was made by a person about whom the public curiosity was for some time strongly excited. It will be recollected, that at the execution of Thistlewood and the rest of the unfortunate wretches who were hanged and decapitated at the Old Bailey for high treason, the man in the black mask and sailor's dress, who suddenly appeared upon the platform with the knife in his hand, and separated each head from the body with so much dexterity was the object of very horrible interest. Various were the surmises about the identity of that individual, who, it was admitted performed his duty as well as Botting [the public hangman] ever did his, but conjecture was quite at fault, until the attempt of which we have spoken was made at the County Gaol of Somersetshire. A short while ago a gentleman named Clarke, who had walked the London Hospitals, was induced by the difficulties which surgeons met with in their search after subjects, to volunteer in the service of the profession at the rate of £12 per head for the dead. He pitched upon one of the most extensive burial grounds in Bath for the scene of his operations, and took a very good house, the back windows of which overlooked into the church-yard, where he was 'to burst the cerements of the sepulchre.' He commenced business in this abode of life and death with wonderful success. The graves gave up their tenants with scarcely the appearance of being violated, but by accident one of the departed was seen moving into Mr Clarke's house one night at the two pair of stairs window. The fact could not long be concealed. The house was searched, and there was no longer any doubting the trade of the proprietor. He was apprehended, and conveyed to Ilchester Gaol, where he represented to his comrades in misfortune, the impropriety of remaining in confinement, when they had an opportunity of going amongst their friends without any restraint.

It is said that his proposal was, that each prisoner should put a stone, or any other heavy article, into his prison stocking (a thick worsted one), and salute the turnkeys with it about the head, if necessary. The inmates of the gaol thought well of this project, and everything was arranged for the cause of liberty. Mr Clarke, however, suddenly repented him of the suggestion, and in the apprehension that murder might be the consequence, very properly intimated to the officers of the prison what was going forward. The intentions of the prisoners were of course completely frustrated. Mr Clarke, to whom the visiting magistrates acknowledged the county was under very great obligations, was requested to state the particulars of his life, and amongst the most interesting, he mentioned that he had presided on the Old Bailey platform with his knife, when Thistlewood died, after Mr Botting had retired with his ropes. We understand that the case of Mr Clarke is to be forthwith represented to the Secretary of State, with the strong recommendation of the County Magistrates.

STAND AND DELIVER!

In March 1879 sixteen-year-old Charlie Cross left the straight and narrow and took young Tommy Hinks with him. Charlie worked as an errand boy for Mr Knight, the Wincanton chemist, and on Thursday, 27 March he was trusted to take £20 in cheques, notes and coins to the bank, but Charlie had other ideas.

Just after half-past-five that afternoon, in company with Tommy Hinks, he arrived at Frank Busby's drapery shop in Milborne Port. Here Charlie bought an overcoat, paying twenty shillings in cash, and Tommy enquired whether there was an ironmonger's shop in the village because he wanted to buy a pistol. The draper, somewhat surprised by the fifteen-years-old's question, said there was not, and at their request he showed the lads the road to Sherborne.

An hour later they entered Mr Bannister's ironmongery in Sherborne and asked the manager, Mr Smith, to show them some revolvers. He took one from the window but Charlie said it was too small. A much larger six-chambered pistol was then produced, and after careful examination Charlie agreed to buy it. The two lads also purchased a quantity of gunpowder, a powder flask, some percussion caps and fifty rounds of ammunition for the pistol. The bill came to 41s 6d which Charlie paid with a £5 note. The pair next called at Woodward and Dorling's drapery where Tommy bought a short, double-breasted coat costing 11s 6d.

At about 7.15pm Mr Hill was working in his saddlery shop in Half Moon Street, when the two youths entered and asked to see some hunting whips. He showed them some which he felt that boys of their class could afford and was a little surprised when they said they wanted something better. Charlie bought a brass-handled whip and Tommy chose one with a bronze handle. In addition each bought a pair of hunting spurs and paid the bill of £1 18s 6d in cash.

Mary Moore was rather frightened by the fierce way the two young men looked at her as she served them beef and cups of tea at Mrs Sansome's refreshment house later that evening. She was relieved when they left after paying the bill of 2s but pleased with the 6d tip they had given her; perhaps they were not so fierce after all.

Shortly before midnight, glove manufacturer Mr George Dyke was returning home on horseback to Milborne Port from South Cheriton. As he cantered along the road from the railway station to Bowden Corner he noticed two figures walking towards him in the gloom and as he drew level with them, the taller of the two shouted

'Stand!' At that moment there was a flash, a loud bang, and Mr Dyke felt a violent blow on his left thigh: he'd been shot! At that same moment the horse bolted and as he galloped down the road, Mr Dyke heard another shot behind him but fortunately this one missed. As he brought the frightened horse under control, his groom James Winter, alerted by the gunfire, came running up the road. Although Winter wanted to pursue the attackers, his master persuaded him not to as they were armed and dangerous. Mr Dyke was a lucky man. When he examined his thigh he found it was only badly bruised. The bullet had entered his overcoat and had been deflected out through the lining by a folded leather strap he kept in his pocket.

Police Constable Devenish of Kington Magna received a call early on Saturday morning informing him that two youths staying overnight in the Ship Inn at West Stour answered the description of the pair wanted for stealing money from Mr Knight of Wincanton. When the officer arrived at the inn he was told the suspects were still in bed. He gave instructions for all outside doors to be locked and then sent the landlady upstairs to tell the youths that breakfast was ready. Charlie and Tommy followed her down straight into the arms of PC Devenish at the bottom. They made no attempt to escape and the officer to searched them without a struggle.

On Charlie Cross, the constable found a cashbook, a £5 note, a purse containing £2 5s 3d in gold and silver, two American coins and, to his surprise, a loaded six-chambered revolver which appeared to have been fired recently as well as 26 rounds of ammunition, a pair of spurs, a whistle, a black mask and false moustache, a cigar holder and three cigars, two pocket knives and a watch.

On Tommy Hinks the astonished policeman found two loaded pistols, one of which appeared to have been fired, a powder flask, some bullets and percussion caps, a pistol ramrod, a black mask and false moustache, a pocket knife, a purse containing £1 4s 11d and he had a rope tied around his waist. Two riding whips were recovered from the room where the two had spent the night.

PC Devenish arrested the youths and they were taken to Shaftesbury police station where, later that day, Sergeant Ottery arrived from Milborne Port. He went straight to the cell occupied by Charlie Cross, cautioned him and charged him with shooting at Mr George Dyke at midnight on 27 March with intent to kill him. Charlie denied the charge and said that he had not left Sherborne till midnight. The sergeant then went to the adjoining cell and charged Tommy Hinks, who having overheard what Charlie had said, told the same story, adding that they had walked through Milborne Port later that night but had seen nobody until they reached Buckhorn Weston at about six o'clock on the Friday morning.

On 4 April the two offenders were brought before the Wincanton magistrates and sent for trial at the spring assizes in Taunton.

When they appeared before the judge, Baron Huddleston, on 29 April, he expressed surprise at the sale of the revolver and ammunition to the youths, but was told that it was not unusual to sell such items to farmers' sons. In his summing up to the jury, the judge pointed out that 'Stand' was a familiar phrase in the literature of the day which did so much damage to lads who enjoyed reading about Dick Turpin and Jack Sheppard.

The jury found both prisoners guilty of shooting with intent to steal but recommended mercy to Tommy Hinks as they considered he had been induced to go with the older Cross. In passing sentence, Baron Huddleston said he had no doubt that what they did was the result of reading books about highwaymen. They had got the idea that it would be a fine thing to have whips and spurs and go around the country committing such offences. He reminded them that if they had been found guilty of shooting at Mr Dyke with intent to kill him he would have sentenced them to penal servitude for life! Instead he was going to give them a chance. The sentences would be not so much to punish them as to set an example to others. The judge believed there was no more effective deterrent than severe and ignominious punishment, namely corporal punishment.

He sentenced Charlie Cross to six months hard labour with thirteen strokes with a birch rod when he entered prison and another thirteen shortly before he was released. Tommy Hinks was given three months and twelve strokes with the birch rod.

There remain a number of questions about this case which the public record leaves unanswered. Where were the two lads on Friday, 28 March between arriving at Buckhorn Weston at 6am after the shooting and taking the room at the Ship Inn that evening? How did they acquire the other two pistols found in their possession? The manager of Mr Bannister's ironmongery only identified the revolver and ammunition as items he had sold to them. And what became of the gunpowder which, according to the record, was never found?

Part of the answer is probably that the two 'highwaymen' spent the Friday acting out their fantasies, firing the weapons in the woods and fields oblivious to the storm that was about to break on their heads. Perhaps one of them stole the two pistols from Bannister's ironmongery when the manager's attention was distracted and he was reluctant to identify the weapons. We shall never know.

FIVE WEIRD STORIES

At the very end of the twentieth century, in our world of instant electric light it is hard to imagine the nineteenth century lit by candles, oil lamps and wavering gas jets, a world of shadows which inspired many a strange and ghostly tale. Let me take you back to that world of shadows and recount some weird Somerset stories.

A Ghostly Instruction

Mr Israel Jesty was a man of some means, he had a thriving shoe-making business in Yeovil, was a widower in his late fifties, and was looking for a wife to share his comfortable home. He believed his search was over in the spring of 1869 when he became engaged to a local widow by the name of Mrs Stickland who, like her suitor, was of reasonable means.

The engagement, unfortunately was not to last and was broken off by the widow, but then a very weird thing happened. The Widow Stickland was sleeping peacefully one night when suddenly she was awoken by three loud knocks which reverberated around the bedroom followed by a strange silence. Then a terrible voice announced in loud and clear tones, 'Israel Jesty is to be thy husband!' Heeding the ghostly instruction, Mrs Stickland immediately renewed her engagement to Mr Jesty and to bind the marriage contract and establish her good faith, she presented her intended with some silver, glass and china articles to the value of £50. This was a fairly substantial sum in the 1860s and was equivalent to a year's wages for a Yeovil glove cutter.

But the marriage never took place because on 21 September 1869, Israel Jesty died at the age of fifty-nine from the heart disease that he had suffered from over the previous two years. Widow Stickland, thus released from the contract, sought the return of the articles she had handed to her fiancé but this was refused by Israel Jesty's heiress, a Mrs Templeman, who claimed that they had belonged to her late father. As quite often happens in such cases, neither side would give in, and Mrs Stickland resorted to the law to obtain the recovery of her treasures. The case was heard in the Court of Exchequer in December 1871 when the plaintiff, Mrs Stickland, claimed that the articles were being wrongfully detained by Mrs Templeman, because they had been lent to Israel Jesty and not given. In her defence, Mrs Templeman stated that Mrs Stickland had asserted that she had been instructed in a vision to take Israel Jesty for her husband, that she had forced him into becoming engaged once more and the disputed articles had been given to bind the new arrangement.

The jury, after hearing the strange tale of the ghostly command, found in favour of Mrs Stickland and awarded damages of £30 against Mrs Templeman, to be reduced to one shilling if the articles were returned. Beware, reader, of ghostly voices giving instructions in the affairs of the heart!

THE DEVIL'S DRIVE

Newton Road leads from Yeovil to Yeovil Junction and climbs up through the wooded slopes of Newton Copse. Above Newton Road stands Summerhouse Hill where a footpath runs between the road and the hill. In the 1893 edition of *Somerset and Dorset Notes and Queries* a contributor, G.F.R. told this story.

In one part of the thickly wooded slopes there is a natural avenue formed in the trees leading from the top of the hill to the road beneath and crossing the footpath at right angles. When I knew it this avenue was quite wide enough to allow a carriage and four to be driven along but it was overgrown with grass and did not appear to have been ever used as a road or way. Moreover it was so steep that it was evident that any ordinary mortal who attempted to drive over it would have come to grief. It was called the 'Devil's Drive' and in the days of my early youth I have often listened in awe to the weird tales that were told me concerning it. It was said that the Devil and some of his kindred spirits were often to be seen at certain hours of the night, and more especially at that witching time 'when churchyards yawn,' taking a drive down over it, and that once on a time one of the townsmen, having occasion to go through the copse in the middle of the night, had suddenly met with his Satanic majesty taking his usual drive. Not only was the townsman very much alarmed at such an unusual spectacle but it seems the spirits did not at all like the interruption. No wonder the Arch fiend turned on the intruder and in very angry tones addressed him thus: 'Walk by day and not by night, And let the spirits take their flight.'

Whether the affrighted townsman profited by this suitable admonition I do not know.

A QUANTOCK HILLS' GHOST

In the 1850s a Miss Williams of Over Stowey had a frightening experience which was recounted by C.H.Sp.P. in the 1891 edition of the *Somerset and Dorset Notes and Queries*:

Miss Williams of Over Stowey was returning home from Watchet late in the evening, when her pony fell and hurt his knees so badly that she was obliged to walk. After proceeding some distance finding it was growing dark, and being 7 or 8 miles from home, she engaged a young countryman at Putsam to accompany her. It soon became very dark and as they were passing through a thick wood and the ground was very wet, and she felt very tired, she again mounted her pony. They had not gone far thus, when she found her pony become suddenly very restive, trembling exceedingly and trying to push sideways through the hedge as if to avoid something. Every effort to make him go on was useless. After a little while, a crashing sound was heard, lasting only a second or two (a kind of clatter like the trucks in Bristol loaded with iron rods). After a few minutes the noise was repeated, still more loudly. The pony was now so ungovernable that Miss W. was obliged to ask the man to hold him by the head. On being asked what the noise was the man seemed much frighted, and said he had never heard anything like it. The noise was repeated a third time and with such an overwhelming crash, that Miss W. felt unable to bear it and stopped her ears. The man was perfectly overpowered with alarm, and sunk to the earth in an agony of fear. Miss W. then observed something approaching which passed close to her, having the appearance of a hearse drawn by four horses, but no one with them and not the slightest sound. On Miss W. asking the man what he had seen, he described exactly the same. After this they neither heard nor saw anything, and the pony went on freely, indeed seemed to hurry homewards. In about half a mile they came to the public house, called the 'Castle of Comfort' where several men were sitting outside the house smoking. Miss W. asked if they had seen anything pass. They said they had not, though they had been sitting there more than an hour and that there was no other way through the wood. They reached Over Stowey about 11, and the young man declared nothing should induce him to pass through that wood again at night, so he remained till morning. The story soon got wind, and some of the older people of the neighbourhood 'wondered how Miss W. could venture to pass through that wood at night', it was so noted for extraordinary noises, &., ever since a dreadful murder of a woman by her husband, who was hung on a gibbet near the spot.

The place of Miss William's ghostly encounter was probably Walford's Gibbet, not far from Over Stowey, where John Walford was executed in 1789 for the murder of his wife.

THE DEAD MAN'S HAND

From the *Western Flying Post* of Monday, 10 May 1831:

In the course of the last fortnight, an inquest was held by Mr Ashford, at the Woolpack Inn, Beckington, on the body of William Halford, a private in the 28th Foot, who met with his death on Sunday, the 1st instant, about midnight, by falling under the wheel of a postchaise. It appeared in evidence that the deceased, with two others, got into a return chaise at Phillip's Norton, which was returning from Bath to Warminster on the evening in question; that the deceased was somewhat stupefied with liquor, and that having alighted at Beckington, he recollected having left his feather and bundle in the postchaise and, running to overtake it, contrived just to catch hold of the handle of the door, by which means he was forced on till he fell under the wheel. Neither the postilion nor the parties inside were in the slightest degree blameable, as the night was very dark, and the unfortunate man had not hallooed the post-boy to stop the vehicle. Verdict Accidental Death. Whilst the body lay in the church, dozens of people, old and young, attended to rub their faces for wens, evil etc. with the dead man's hand.

BURIED ALIVE?

Many Victorians had a morbid dread of being buried alive and no doubt some readers of the *Western Gazette and Flying Post* of 4 March 1870, felt a cold shudder run down their spine at the following report:

Merriott

Buried Alive

A rumour has been circulated that Richard Parsons, whose death we recorded last week, was buried alive on Monday last. The sexton states that as he was filling in the grave he heard a groan, as if proceeding from the coffin. He did not, however, take any notice of it but filled in the grave. Deceased had been ill for three months and died as was supposed on the 17th. He was placed in his coffin, the lid of which was screwed down, about four hours before the burial. The matter is to be investigated by the Parish authorities.

No doubt to the relief of readers with a delicate disposition it appears the story had no foundation because no further action is reported.

THE 1885 GENERAL ELECTION

The log book of Reckleford School in Yeovil records for the week ending 11 December 1885, that 'Attendance for this week was 10 less than the previous week owing to the Parliamentary Election on Tuesday and many parents keeping their children home due to the disturbed state of the town.'

In 1885 the southern part of Somerset was divided into two parliamentary constituencies or divisions; South-east Somerset and South Somerset. Polling took place on different days in 1885, in South-east Somerset it was on 27 November and in South Somerset on 8 December; in each case the counting of the votes and the declaration of the results was held on the following day.

Henry Hobhouse was declared the winner of the South-east Somerset poll in Shepton Mallet on 28 November. Reporting on the announcement of the election of Mr Hobhouse, a local newspaper was relieved to inform its readers that Shepton Mallet was unusually quiet on Saturday and only one or two noteworthy incidents occurred. Two shop windows were broken but, as the reporter observed, 'by whom or for what reason is not known as there was not even a crowd near at the time.' Likewise in Castle Cary, to the apparent surprise of the commentator, polling day passed with an entire absence of disorder or undue excitement. Considerable amazement was caused in the area by the importing of a number of police constables and one tradesman was 'chaffed' for barricading his windows. Bruton and Milborne Port were both quiet.

However, in Langport things were a little different. Polling day passed quietly enough, with a good turnout of 451 voters out of an electoral roll of 514; in 1885 most women had no right to vote and and because of the property qualification rules neither did quite a few men. The poll closed at 8pm and a large number of boys and men gathered outside the polling station at the Board School and threw stones and dirt at leading local politicians. Sticks were also used and it was some time before the constabulary could restore order. The burghers of Somerton, just down the road, no doubt breathed a sight of relief when the poll closed in an orderly manner and so election day in South-east Somerset closed with little evidence of the feared disturbance.

But South Somerset would be going to the polls on 8 December, and there was plenty of time for the agitators and disaffected to get to work. As darkness fell on 8 December, a crowd of boys paraded the streets of Yeovil, and although a few house windows were smashed, no damage was caused to shop windows as originally feared. Many of the shops had been heavily barricaded but the large contingent of police patrolling the town kept the peace and by midnight everything was quiet.

The following day counting started in the town hall at eleven o'clock, by which time most of the shops in High Street, Hendford and Princes Street had closed and were barricaded once again. The large police presence kept the trouble-makers away and apart from a little shouting and heckling from the crowd at the declaration of Lord Kilcoursie's victory, the rest of the day passed peacefully.

In Crewkerne, some sixty to seventy volunteer special constables, referred to by one disgruntled local as the 'rolling pin brigade,' were sworn in to keep the peace on election day. Crewkerne recorded a very high poll as well as a large number of county police on duty. Once again the feared rioting did not occur and the only trouble came from a few unruly special constables who got very drunk and had to be 'disbanded' for the protection of their fellow specials! One of the volunteer specials, described as being worth two pressed men, was found lying dead drunk before the poll closed.

In Chard, the measures taken by the Borough Watch Committee and the county magistrates to preserve the peace proved to be effective and election day passed off without trouble. No doubt the presence of 50 regular police from Bristol, and the 100 special constables, was sufficient to overawe any would-be rioters.

Throughout the rest of the South Somerset constituency Martock, Ilchester, Stoke-sub-Hamdon, Montacute and West Coker were all quiet and no disturbances were reported from Ilminster where in previous years there had been some rioting. In Curry Rivel, like its neighbour Langport during the previous week, it was not so quiet. At the close of poll 'roughs' began to congregate at the crossroads and a Mr Knowles, who was driving through the village to collect the ballot boxes, was stoned, and both head lamps of his pony trap were smashed. Windows were broken throughout the village and the vicarage was subjected to a concentrated stoning. The local constabulary, which was thinly stretched, took some time to restore order.

So passed the general election of 1885 without the wholesale rioting feared by the parents of the pupils of Reckleford School and no doubt to the relief of the majority of law-abiding Somerset folk.

THE SKIMMINGTON

There was a form of rough justice exercised by our ancestors known as the skimmington, riding the skimmington or skimmerton, or riding the stang. There were many other local dialect variations of the name that stretched back into the mists of time.

On the north wall of the Great Hall at Montacute House there are two early seventeenth-century plasterwork panels which depict a henpecked husband having a quick drink of ale while he baby-sits. He is set upon by his wife and a neighbour who witnesses the scene tells the village. The husband is then depicted 'riding the skimmington', sitting on a pole and being paraded around the village to the jeers of his neighbours.

The skimmington sometimes took the form of men and youths parading in front of an offender's house and making 'rough music' by beating kettles, trays, buckets and anything else which would make a loud noise. Although generally harmless, the resulting stigma could lead to a family or individual moving away and, on occasion, the event could get out of hand.

One such incident occurred in Yeovil on 5 April 1827 when a crowd of over a hundred men, women and youths gathered outside the cottage of Thomazine Hawker, a lady of alleged easy virtue, and began a 'rough band' on flutes, kettles and pans. Thomazine Hawker came to her door and, as she stepped outside, John Mabey, one of the ringleaders of the mob, shouted, 'There goes the whore!', a cry taken up by John Collins who yelled, 'Let's play the Whore's Tune!' A stone crashed against one of the window shutters and more missiles followed as the unfortunate Thomazine fled back indoors.

The 'rough band' continued to play for another two hours until the town constables finally dispersed the mob. John Mabey and John Collins were arrested and put on trial at the Easter Quarter Sessions charged with 'having been with divers other persons riotously assembled and assaulted and ill-treated Thomazine Hawker.' Despite glowing character references from the mens' employer, George Harris, builder and carpenter, they were found guilty and sent down for six months hard labour in the county gaol.

Riding the skimmington could be physically cruel as shown in another case which occurred in Yeovil nearly twenty years later in May 1845. On this occasion some building workers employed by a Mr Stent accused one of their number, Tyrus Hockey, of stealing their dinners of bread and bacon. To teach him a lesson and make an example, the men sat Hockey on a rafter and tied a board to his back upon which the words 'A THIF' were scrawled. Hockey's limbs were bound and the rafter, with its passenger, was lifted on to the men's shoulders and the skimmington rode through the streets of the town. One of the local newspapers reported that the 'lynchers who had recreated this almost obsolete punishment had contrived to refine the cruelty of the punishment by sharpening the point of the rafter on which the unfortunate fellow sat and by jagging him at several places.'

The town police eventually stopped the proceedings and Tyrus Hockey was lifted off. He was so badly bruised that he had to be taken home to Bradford Abbas in a cart and was under medical care for two days. Eleven men were arrested and brought before the town magistrates on the 5 June, charged with riot and assault. All were bound over in their individual recognizances of 4s 6d to appear at the next Quarter Sessions. The magistrates were very critical of the absence of the town police during the one and a half hours when the skimmington was being ridden, and considered it 'monstrous that during that time not one of that body was to be found.' Perhaps, on this occasion, there was some sympathy with the builders and discretion was the better part of valour.

At the Quarter Sessions, all eleven men received prison sentences ranging from three days to six weeks.

YEOVIL CEMETERY
HOLDS A SECRET

In Yeovil Cemetery there lie three unknown people whose lives were ended in a split second by a German bomb in the autumn of 1940. The stark headstone reads:

OCTOBER 1940
THREE AIR RAID VICTIMS
KNOWN UNTO GOD

Who were these unknown people? All were so mutilated that no identification was possible but it was established that one was an adult female and one a small child of between one and three years of age. The age and sex of the third could not be determined.

In July in the summer of 1940, when Great Britain held its breath and waited for the onslaught of Hitler's Third Reich, air raid sirens first wailed across Yeovil. From that day until 7 October there were 32 alerts but, although everyone knew that the Westland Aircraft Works would sooner or later become a target, mercifully no bombs had fallen on the town. The thirty-third alert at quarter-to-four in the afternoon on Monday, 7 October was, however, very different. The Luftwaffe had finally come to Yeovil with a vengeance. More than 25 bombers attacked the Westland works but no damage was caused to the factory for the assault fell on the town centre and nearby residential areas. A direct hit demolished the air raid shelter at the Methodist church in Vicarage Street; Burton's shop in Middle Street was destroyed and houses in the area of Summerleaze Park, St Andrew's Road, Grove Avenue, and the Higher Kingston Estate were hit. When the all clear sounded an hour later, seven men and nine women had died in the attack and over forty were wounded.

The Luftwaffe came again the next evening and between 7.10 and 7.50 scattered bombs over the town. Once again the residential areas took the full weight of the attack. An air raid shelter at the corner of Preston Grove and Westbourne Grove received a direct hit and all its occupants were killed.

Eight of those who died in the raid were soon identified and by the end of that devastating evening it was believed that all had been accounted for. However, on the following morning, two badly mutilated bodies were found in the Preston Grove area: one was a child, but the age and sex of the other could not be established. On 13 October the remains of a woman were found on a nearby allotment but once again, identification was not possible.

There were no reports of any missing persons among local residents and on 15 October, the three unknown casualties were buried in Yeovil cemetery. The child was given a number, 15; the adult female, number 23, and the unidentifiable victim, number 17.

Who were numbers 15, 23 and 17? At that time Yeovil was home, as were many other towns, to hundreds of women and children evacuated from London and other major cities. On 14 October 1940 the estimated civil population of the town was 25,000, made up of 20,000 pre-war general residents, 3800 war workers and their families, 1350 officially billeted evacuees and 350 refugees and unofficial evacuees.

A letter from the town clerk dated 14 October 1940, six days after the attack, to an enquirer in Lincoln, illustrates the problem of trying to keep check on the hundreds of evacuees and refugees:

> With reference to your telegram of yesterday's date I regret that I have so far been unable to trace the present address of your sister... The house which she occupied at 35 St Andrew's Road, Yeovil was only slightly damaged during a recent air raid but she appears to have left the premises without acquainting the Council of the address to which she has gone.

The record does not disclose if the clerk traced this lady.

Another letter to a lady in Wilton, on 16 October reads:

> In reply to your letter received this morning concerning your friend Mrs Burgess and her daughter Eva, I regret that I am unable to furnish you with their present address. I have no one of that name billeted in this town, and since you do not give me their home address I have insufficient information concerning these people to enable me to ask other authorities to help in tracing them. I suggest you contact the County Council at Taunton.

Did someone wonder what happened to a relation, neighbour or friend who never returned? Or was there no one left anywhere to speculate on what had happened to someone they had once known? The mystery remains in Yeovil cemetery where three human beings, their names known only to God, have their last resting place by a spreading fir tree.

SOURCES

THE LOSS OF THE *WILLIAM AND MARY*
Cheltenham and Gloucester Gazette, 29 October and 5 November 1817.
Bath Chronicle, 30 October and 6 and 20 November 1817.
The Times, 28 October and 1, 4 and 13 November 1817.
Western Flying Post, 3 November and 1 December 1817.
Taunton Courier, 6 November and 4 December 1817.
Felix Farley's Bristol Journal, 15 November 1817.
Bristol Mirror, 1, 8 and 15 November 1817.

THE BRUTES OF BRIDGWATER
Taunton Courier, 29 January and 16 April 1823.
Western Flying Post, 27 January and 3 February 1823.

A LIFE LOST FOR A KISS
Western Flying Post, 26 August 1857.

WESTON PIER DESTROYED BY FIRE
Western Gazette, 17 January 1930.

THE SHOOTING AT THE ROCK HOUSE INN
Western Flying Post, 22 and 29 August 1814.
Taunton Courier, 26 May, 25 August and 1 September 1814.

THE SOUTH SOMERSET BREAD RIOTS
J.W. Sweet, *South Somerset News and Views*, October 1994 and
January 1995.

A PROPHECY OF DISASTER
J.W. Sweet, *South Somerset News and Views*, April 1993.

THE SHOOTING OF LORD GLASTONBURY'S GAMEKEEPER
J.W. Sweet, *South Somerset News and Views*, March 1997.

BAD BLOOD IN LEIGH-ON-MENDIP
Somerset and Wilts Journal, 3, 10 and 17 October 1857, 27 March and 3
April 1858.
Western Flying Post, 6, 13 and 20 October 1857, 6 April 1858.

A SHORT STEP AND A LONG DROP
J.W. Sweet, *South Somerset News and Views*, March 1995.

THE ERRAND BOY'S COURAGE
J.W. Sweet, *South Somerset News and Views*, January 1996.

THE MURDER OF INNOCENTS
Western Flying Post, 27 January, 10 November and
29 December 1857.
Western Gazette and Flying Post, 11 June 1869.
Western Gazette and Flying Post, 28 January, 11 February and 27 May 1870.
1861 Census Return.   Queen Camel RG/1647, Yeovil Reference Library.

THE QUACK DOCTOR FROM CREWKERNE.
J.W. Sweet, *South Somerset News and Views*, August 1995.

THE FALL OF A WYVERN
Western Gazette, 4 November and 16 December 1949.

TAUNTON'S MAD MUNICIPAL MOMENTS
Western Gazette, 14 August 1896 and 13 February 1903.

THE DAY THE BALLOON DIDN'T GO UP
J.W. Sweet, *South Somerset News and Views*, May 1997.

OF MURDERERS AND HIGHWAYMEN
J.W. Sweet, *South Somerset News and Views*, November 1995.

THE THRASHING OF PROFESSOR WHITWORTH
J.W. Sweet, *South Somerset News and Views*, October 1996.

THE STRANGE CASE OF THE POISONED BABY OF BATH
Western Flying Post, 14 and 21 October 1851, 6 April 1852.
Taunton Courier, 22 October 1851.
The Bath Chronicle, 8 April 1852.

THE BLIZZARD OF 1891
Western Gazette, 13 March and 3 April 1891.

A DASTARDLY OUTRAGE
Western Gazette, 28 January, 1910.

PLAYING CARDS ON SUNDAY
Western Gazette, 7 November 1890.

AN OCTOBER STORM
Western Flying Post, 1 November 1859.
The Somerset Year Book 1926, page 108.

RICHARD HEWLETT – UNSUCCESSFUL HIGHWAYMAN
Western Flying Post, 1 November 1830, 11, 16 and 25 April 1831.
Taunton Courier, 6 April 1831.

LOVE THY NEIGHBOUR
Western Gazette, 9 January 1903.

THE MAYOR FLIES TO BRISTOL
J.W. Sweet, *South Somerset News and Views*, June 1996.

THE FATAL FIRING
J.W. Sweet, *South Somerset News and Views*, July 1996.

EIGHT ESCAPE FROM PLYMOUTH
Western Flying Post, 27 January and 3 February 1823.

ARSENIC AND CANDY – A MYSTERY
Somerset and Wilts Journal, 1 September 1855.
The Bath Chronicle, 16, 23 and 30 August 1855.
Western Flying Post, 28 August and 4 September 1855.
Taunton Courier, 15 and 29 August 1855.

THE TRAGEDY ON THE WEYMOUTH EXCURSION
J.W. Sweet, *South Somerset News and Views*, August 1991.
The Western Gazette, 3 October 1913.

SOMETHING IN THE ATTIC
Western Gazette, 4 and 11 September 1896.
Langport and Somerton Herald, 5 and 12 September 1896.

THE HOMICIDAL SERVANT GIRL
Western Flying Post, 21 April 1827.

MR MORFORD AND THE GERMAN SPY
Western Gazette, 21 August 1914.

THE PASSING OF TREVOR HOYLE
J.W. Sweet, unpublished papers.

A GAOL BREAK FOILED AND A MYSTERY SOLVED, PERHAPS
Taunton Courier, 8 February 1827.

STAND AND DELIVER!
J.W. Sweet, *South Somerset News and Views*, March 1993.

FIVE WEIRD STORIES
A Ghostly Instruction
Western Gazette and Flying Post, 29 December 1871.
The Devil's Drive
Somerset and Dorset Notes and Queries 1893, p.130.
A Quantock Hills' Ghost
Somerset and Dorset Notes and Queries 1891, p.242.
The Deadman's Hand
Western Flying Post, 10 May 1831.
Buried Alive?
Western Gazette and Flying Post, 4 March 1870.

THE 1885 GENERAL ELECTION
J.W. Sweet, *The Visitor Magazine*, April 1992.

THE SKIMMINGTON
J.W. Sweet, *South Somerset News and Views*, April 1997.

YEOVIL CEMETERY HOLDS A SECRET
J.W. Sweet, unpublished papers.